PETER
THE GREAT

PETER THE GREAT

Kathleen McDermott

CHELSEA HOUSE PUBLISHERS
NEW YORK
PHILADELPHIA

Chelsea House Publishers
EDITOR-IN-CHIEF: Remmel Nunn
MANAGING EDITOR: Karyn Gullen Browne
COPY CHIEF: Juliann Barbato
PICTURE EDITOR: Adrian G. Allen
ART DIRECTOR: Maria Epes
DEPUTY COPY CHIEF: Mark Rifkin
ASSISTANT ART DIRECTOR: Loraine Machlin
MANUFACTURING MANAGER: Gerald Levine
PRODUCTION MANAGER: Joseph Romano
PRODUCTION COORDINATOR: Marie Claire Cebrián

World Leaders—Past & Present
SENIOR EDITOR: John Selfridge

Staff for PETER THE GREAT
ASSOCIATE EDITOR: Terrance Dolan
COPY EDITOR: Brian Sookram
EDITORIAL ASSISTANT: Martin Mooney
PICTURE RESEARCHER: Lisa Kirchner
DESIGNER: David Murray
COVER ILLUSTRATION: Daniel Mark Duffy

3 5 7 9 8 6 4

Library of Congress Cataloging-in-Publication Data

McDermott, Kathleen.
    Peter the Great/Kathleen McDermott.
    p.   cm.—(World leaders past & present)
    Includes bibliographical references.
    Summary: A biography of the czar who began the transformation of
Russia into a modern state in the late seventeenth–early eighteenth
centuries.
    ISBN 1-55546-821-7
        0-7910-0703-0 (pbk.)
    1. Peter I, Emperor of Russia, 1672–1725—Juvenile literature.
2. Soviet Union—Kings and rulers—Biography—Juvenile literature.
3. Soviet Union—History—Peter I, 1689–1725—Juvenile literature. [1.
Peter I, Emperor of Russia, 1672–1725. 2. Kings, queens, rulers, etc.
3. Soviet Union—History—Peter I, 1689—1725.] I. Title. II. Series.
DK131.M37   1990
947′.05′092—dc20   90–1791
[B]   CIP
[92]   AC

Contents

John Adams
John Quincy Adams
Konrad Adenauer
Alexander the Great
Salvador Allende
Marc Antony
Corazon Aquino
Yasir Arafat
King Arthur
Hafez al-Assad
Kemal Atatürk
Attila
Clement Attlee
Augustus Caesar
Menachem Begin
David Ben-Gurion
Otto von Bismarck
Léon Blum
Simon Bolívar
Cesare Borgia
Willy Brandt
Leonid Brezhnev
Julius Caesar
John Calvin
Jimmy Carter
Fidel Castro
Catherine the Great
Charlemagne
Chiang Kai-Shek
Winston Churchill
Georges Clemenceau
Cleopatra
Constantine the Great
Hernán Cortés
Oliver Cromwell
Georges-Jacques
    Danton
Jefferson Davis
Moshe Dayan
Charles de Gaulle
Eamon De Valera
Eugene Debs
Deng Xiaoping
Benjamin Disraeli
Alexander Dubček
François & Jean-Claude
    Duvalier
Dwight Eisenhower
Eleanor of Aquitaine
Elizabeth I
Faisal
Ferdinand & Isabella
Francisco Franco
Benjamin Franklin

Frederick the Great
Indira Gandhi
Mohandas Gandhi
Giuseppe Garibaldi
Amin & Bashir Gemayel
Genghis Khan
William Gladstone
Mikhail Gorbachev
Ulysses S. Grant
Ernesto "Che" Guevara
Tenzin Gyatso
Alexander Hamilton
Dag Hammarskjöld
Henry VIII
Henry of Navarre
Paul von Hindenburg
Hirohito
Adolf Hitler
Ho Chi Minh
King Hussein
Ivan the Terrible
Andrew Jackson
James I
Wojciech Jaruzelski
Thomas Jefferson
Joan of Arc
Pope John XXIII
Pope John Paul II
Lyndon Johnson
Benito Juárez
John Kennedy
Robert Kennedy
Jomo Kenyatta
Ayatollah Khomeini
Nikita Khrushchev
Kim Il Sung
Martin Luther King, Jr.
Henry Kissinger
Kublai Khan
Lafayette
Robert E. Lee
Vladimir Lenin
Abraham Lincoln
David Lloyd George
Louis XIV
Martin Luther
Judas Maccabeus
James Madison
Nelson & Winnie
    Mandela
Mao Zedong
Ferdinand Marcos
George Marshall

Mary, Queen of Scots
Tomáš Masaryk
Golda Meir
Klemens von Metternich
James Monroe
Hosni Mubarak
Robert Mugabe
Benito Mussolini
Napoléon Bonaparte
Gamal Abdel Nasser
Jawaharlal Nehru
Nero
Nicholas II
Richard Nixon
Kwame Nkrumah
Daniel Ortega
Mohammed Reza Pahlavi
Thomas Paine
Charles Stewart
    Parnell
Pericles
Juan Perón
Peter the Great
Pol Pot
Muammar el-Qaddafi
Ronald Reagan
Cardinal Richelieu
Maximilien Robespierre
Eleanor Roosevelt
Franklin Roosevelt
Theodore Roosevelt
Anwar Sadat
Haile Selassie
Prince Sihanouk
Jan Smuts
Joseph Stalin
Sukarno
Sun Yat-sen
Tamerlane
Mother Teresa
Margaret Thatcher
Josip Broz Tito
Toussaint L'Ouverture
Leon Trotsky
Pierre Trudeau
Harry Truman
Queen Victoria
Lech Walesa
George Washington
Chaim Weizmann
Woodrow Wilson
Xerxes
Emiliano Zapata
Zhou Enlai

CHELSEA HOUSE PUBLISHERS

ON LEADERSHIP

Arthur M. Schlesinger, jr.

LEADERSHIP, it may be said, is really what makes the world go round. Love no doubt smooths the passage; but love is a private transaction between consenting adults. Leadership is a public transaction with history. The idea of leadership affirms the capacity of individuals to move, inspire, and mobilize masses of people so that they act together in pursuit of an end. Sometimes leadership serves good purposes, sometimes bad; but whether the end is benign or evil, great leaders are those men and women who leave their personal stamp on history.

Now, the very concept of leadership implies the proposition that individuals can make a difference. This proposition has never been universally accepted. From classical times to the present day, eminent thinkers have regarded individuals as no more than the agents and pawns of larger forces, whether the gods and goddesses of the ancient world or, in the modern era, race, class, nation, the dialectic, the will of the people, the spirit of the times, history itself. Against such forces, the individual dwindles into insignificance.

So contends the thesis of historical determinism. Tolstoy's great novel *War and Peace* offers a famous statement of the case. Why, Tolstoy asked, did millions of men in the Napoleonic Wars, denying their human feelings and their common sense, move back and forth across Europe slaughtering their fellows? "The war," Tolstoy answered, "was bound to happen simply because it was bound to happen." All prior history predetermined it. As for leaders, they, Tolstoy said, "are but the labels that serve to give a name to an end and, like labels, they have the least possible connection with the event." The greater the leader, "the more conspicuous the inevitability and the predestination of every act he commits." The leader, said Tolstoy, is "the slave of history."

Determinism takes many forms. Marxism is the determinism of class. Nazism the determinism of race. But the idea of men and women as the slaves of history runs athwart the deepest human instincts. Rigid determinism abolishes the idea of human freedom—

the assumption of free choice that underlies every move we make, every word we speak, every thought we think. It abolishes the idea of human responsibility, since it is manifestly unfair to reward or punish people for actions that are by definition beyond their control. No one can live consistently by any deterministic creed. The Marxist states prove this themselves by their extreme susceptibility to the cult of leadership.

More than that, history refutes the idea that individuals make no difference. In December 1931 a British politician crossing Park Avenue in New York City between 76th and 77th Streets around 10:30 P.M. looked in the wrong direction and was knocked down by an automobile—a moment, he later recalled, of a man aghast, a world aglare: "I do not understand why I was not broken like an eggshell or squashed like a gooseberry." Fourteen months later an American politician, sitting in an open car in Miami, Florida, was fired on by an assassin; the man beside him was hit. Those who believe that individuals make no difference to history might well ponder whether the next two decades would have been the same had Mario Constasino's car killed Winston Churchill in 1931 and Giuseppe Zangara's bullet killed Franklin Roosevelt in 1933. Suppose, in addition, that Adolf Hitler had been killed in the street fighting during the Munich *Putsch* of 1923 and that Lenin had died of typhus during World War I. What would the 20th century be like now?

For better or for worse, individuals do make a difference. "The notion that a people can run itself and its affairs anonymously," wrote the philosopher William James, "is now well known to be the silliest of absurdities. Mankind does nothing save through initiatives on the part of inventors, great or small, and imitation by the rest of us—these are the sole factors in human progress. Individuals of genius show the way, and set the patterns, which common people then adopt and follow."

Leadership, James suggests, means leadership in thought as well as in action. In the long run, leaders in thought may well make the greater difference to the world. But, as Woodrow Wilson once said, "Those only are leaders of men, in the general eye, who lead in action. . . . It is at their hands that new thought gets its translation into the crude language of deeds." Leaders in thought often invent in solitude and obscurity, leaving to later generations the tasks of imitation. Leaders in action—the leaders portrayed in this series—have to be effective in their own time.

And they cannot be effective by themselves. They must act in response to the rhythms of their age. Their genius must be adapted, in a phrase of William James's, "to the receptivities of the moment." Leaders are useless without followers. "There goes the mob," said the French politician hearing a clamor in the streets. "I am their leader. I must follow them." Great leaders turn the inchoate emotions of the mob to purposes of their own. They seize on the opportunities of their time, the hopes, fears, frustrations, crises, potentialities. They succeed when events have prepared the way for them, when the community is awaiting to be aroused, when they can provide the clarifying and organizing ideas. Leadership ignites the circuit between the individual and the mass and thereby alters history.

It may alter history for better or for worse. Leaders have been responsible for the most extravagant follies and most monstrous crimes that have beset suffering humanity. They have also been vital in such gains as humanity has made in individual freedom, religious and racial tolerance, social justice, and respect for human rights.

There is no sure way to tell in advance who is going to lead for good and who for evil. But a glance at the gallery of men and women in *World Leaders—Past and Present* suggests some useful tests.

One test is this: Do leaders lead by force or by persuasion? By command or by consent? Through most of history leadership was exercised by the divine right of authority. The duty of followers was to defer and to obey. "Theirs not to reason why / Theirs but to do and die." On occasion, as with the so-called enlightened despots of the 18th century in Europe, absolutist leadership was animated by humane purposes. More often, absolutism nourished the passion for domination, land, gold, and conquest and resulted in tyranny.

The great revolution of modern times has been the revolution of equality. The idea that all people should be equal in their legal condition has undermined the old structure of authority, hierarchy, and deference. The revolution of equality has had two contrary effects on the nature of leadership. For equality, as Alexis de Tocqueville pointed out in his great study *Democracy in America*, might mean equality in servitude as well as equality in freedom.

"I know of only two methods of establishing equality in the political world," Tocqueville wrote. "Rights must be given to every citizen, or none at all to anyone . . . save one, who is the master of all." There was no middle ground "between the sovereignty of all and the absolute power of one man." In his astonishing prediction of 20th-century totalitarian dictatorship, Tocqueville explained how the revolution of equality could lead to the *"Führerprinzip"* and more terrible absolutism than the world had ever known.

But when rights are given to every citizen and the sovereignty of all is established, the problem of leadership takes a new form, becomes more exacting than ever before. It is easy to issue commands and enforce them by the rope and the stake, the concentration camp and the *gulag.* It is much harder to use argument and achievement to overcome opposition and win consent. The Founding Fathers of the United States understood the difficulty. They believed that history had given them the opportunity to decide, as Alexander Hamilton wrote in the first Federalist Paper, whether men are indeed capable of basing government on "reflection and choice, or whether they are forever destined to depend . . . on accident and force."

Government by reflection and choice called for a new style of leadership and a new quality of followership. It required leaders to be responsive to popular concerns, and it required followers to be active and informed participants in the process. Democracy does not eliminate emotion from politics; sometimes it fosters demagoguery; but it is confident that, as the greatest of democratic leaders put it, you cannot fool all of the people all of the time. It measures leadership by results and retires those who overreach or falter or fail.

It is true that in the long run despots are measured by results too. But they can postpone the day of judgment, sometimes indefinitely, and in the meantime they can do infinite harm. It is also true that democracy is no guarantee of virtue and intelligence in government, for the voice of the people is not necessarily the voice of God. But democracy, by assuring the right of opposition, offers built-in resistance to the evils inherent in absolutism. As the theologian Reinhold Niebuhr summed it up, "Man's capacity for justice makes democracy possible, but man's inclination to injustice makes democracy necessary."

A second test for leadership is the end for which power is sought. When leaders have as their goal the supremacy of a master race or the promotion of totalitarian revolution or the acquisition and exploitation of colonies or the protection of greed and privilege or the preservation of personal power, it is likely that their leadership will do little to advance the cause of humanity. When their goal is the abolition of slavery, the liberation of women, the enlargement of opportunity for the poor and powerless, the extension of equal rights to racial minorities, the defense of the freedoms of expression and opposition, it is likely that their leadership will increase the sum of human liberty and welfare.

Leaders have done great harm to the world. They have also conferred great benefits. You will find both sorts in this series. Even "good" leaders must be regarded with a certain wariness. Leaders are not demigods; they put on their trousers one leg after another just like ordinary mortals. No leader is infallible, and every leader needs to be reminded of this at regular intervals. Irreverence irritates leaders but is their salvation. Unquestioning submission corrupts leaders and demeans followers. Making a cult of a leader is always a mistake. Fortunately hero worship generates its own antidote. "Every hero," said Emerson, "becomes a bore at last."

The signal benefit the great leaders confer is to embolden the rest of us to live according to our own best selves, to be active, insistent, and resolute in affirming our own sense of things. For great leaders attest to the reality of human freedom against the supposed inevitabilities of history. And they attest to the wisdom and power that may lie within the most unlikely of us, which is why Abraham Lincoln remains the supreme example of great leadership. A great leader, said Emerson, exhibits new possibilities to all humanity. "We feed on genius. . . . Great men exist that there may be greater men."

Great leaders, in short, justify themselves by emancipating and empowering their followers. So humanity struggles to master its destiny, remembering with Alexis de Tocqueville: "It is true that around every man a fatal circle is traced beyond which he cannot pass; but within the wide verge of that circle he is powerful and free; as it is with man, so with communities."

1
A Contest of Wills

As Sweden's warrior-king Charles XII pushed across the Russian frontier with his army of 42,000 troops, the Russians retreated before him. Czar Peter had issued strict orders that the Russians were not to engage Charles in a pitched battle; instead, Peter's forces withdrew deeper and deeper into the vast Russian interior, burning the land around them as they went in order to deprive the Swedes of food and fodder. Peter was waiting for the arrival of his most powerful ally. It was not the friendly armies of Poland or Denmark that Peter was awaiting; rather, it was a force that had been used by Russian commanders throughout history to turn back foreign invasions; a force that was to defeat, long after Peter's time, the armies of Napoleon and Hitler. It was the Russian winter — cold, harsh, and unforgiving.

All across Europe, the winter of 1708–9 was the most bitter anyone could remember. In Paris, the Seine iced up, and the wine in the royal cellars froze.

Taller than all the courtiers, the young Czar draws the greatest attention to his person. His intelligence and his knowledge of military affairs are developing as auspiciously as his physical qualities.

—VAN KELLER
Dutch envoy to
Moscow, 1688

Czar Peter the Great, Russia's willful, savage, and visionary leader, ruled from 1682 to 1725. During that time, Peter transformed his country from an isolated, backward kingdom into a dominant power in Europe.

King Charles XII of Sweden, a brilliant and fearless warrior, launched an invasion of Russia in January 1708. The Russians fell back before making a final stand at the small town of Poltava on July 8.

Ice floated in the canals of Venice. A brutal cold fell upon the vast plains of the Ukraine, and raging, icy winds turned the landscape into a barren, polar wasteland. Temperatures plummeted, blizzards howled, Peter's armies fell back, and Charles pursued them. The dauntless king of Sweden and his men had been lured into an icy trap.

Charles fumed as his men froze and his supplies dwindled: If only the Russians would turn and fight. When he heard a report that they were massing outside the walled town of Gadyach, 35 miles from the Swedish encampment, Charles ordered his army to form for battle, and they quickly closed in on the Russians. The Russians let the Swedes draw close, then suddenly dispersed into the woods like a winter mirage. The frustrated Swedes had no choice but to continue on to Gadyach for shelter — night was falling, the temperature was well below zero, and they were too far from their previous encampment to turn back. But Gadyach had only one small entrance, and the bulk of the Swedish army had to wait up to three days — and nights — to get in. Left outside at night, with no shelter, more than 3,000 Swedish soldiers froze to death. Most of the survivors were damaged by severe frostbite, losing noses, fingers, toes, and ears. Charles comforted himself with the thought that the Russian soldiers had to be suffering the same way. The Russians, however, were fully supplied with winter clothing, and they were safely encamped during the worst of the weather.

The two armies continued their dance. The Swedes were in a miserable state: They were hungry and freezing, their uniforms in tatters, their boots full of holes. Many had been crippled by the cold. Charles was forced to halt the march in late February 1709, when heavy rainfall and melting snow turned the countryside into a sea of mud. His officers tried to persuade the obstinate young king to make for Poland, where he could safely rest his men and get reinforcements and provisions. But Charles would not admit defeat, and his army pushed on. By early spring the first Swedish troops had reached the town of Poltava, 200 miles southeast of Kiev. Charles decided to capture the town. Having let the Russian winter take its toll of the Swedes, Peter led his army toward Poltava and his archenemy.

On June 17, Charles's 27th birthday, the king was inspecting his front line when he was shot by a Russian sniper. The musket ball ripped through Charles's left foot. Bone splinters had to be surgically removed, and the wound began to fester. It was a heavy blow to the Swedes, who had always believed that their commander, up to now unscathed in battle, was protected by God. For days Charles lay in a fever, and many feared he was near death. Hearing the news, Peter quickly moved his troops into an advantageous position outside Poltava.

By June 22, Charles had come out of his fever. To pick up his men's morale, the king had himself carried before them on a stretcher. With Charles on his back, his generals urged him to negotiate peace with Peter. The proud Charles refused, and just before the sun rose on June 28, 1709, the Battle of Poltava began. It would prove to be the decisive confrontation of the Great Northern War. In the pre-dawn twilight, waiting nervously for the order to attack, Swedish soldiers in the front lines may well have caught a glimpse of their tormentor as he rode up and down his own lines, giving final words of encouragement to his men. Astride his magnificent dun Arabian, the gigantic Peter wore the red-trimmed green coat of the Preobrazhenskoe Regiment, high black boots, and a black three-cornered hat. Across his chest was the blue ribbon of the Order of St. Andrew; inside his jacket, an ancient silver icon hung from his neck. (According to legend, the silver icon stopped a Swedish bullet during the battle.) The czar was at last ready to face Charles.

Peter the Great leads the Russian army to victory over the Swedish forces of Charles XII at the Battle of Poltava. Following the battle, Peter proclaimed, "Now the final stone has been laid of the foundation of St. Petersburg."

The battle raged throughout the morning, and by noon the outcome was clear: Charles's army was in full retreat and the field was littered with 7,000 Swedish dead and wounded. The Russians had taken nearly 3,000 prisoners. The survivors, including Charles, headed south, hoping to find refuge with the Turks. While the Swedes fled, Peter held a joyous thanksgiving service in his camp. At dinner with his generals, the czar ordered the captured Swedish officers brought to him. He saluted their courage. As the celebration continued into the night, Peter found time to write to his wife, Catherine: "I declare to you that the all-merciful God has this day granted us an unprecedented victory over the enemy. In a word, the whole of the enemy's army is knocked on the head. . . . P.S. Come here and congratulate us." Soon, all of Europe would know of Russia's triumph and would recognize that there was a new power in the land.

Natalya Naryshkina became caught up in a rivalry with the family of her husband's first wife, Mariya Miloslavskaya. The feud resulted in bloodshed.

Early on the morning of May 30, 1672, Czar Alexis I Mikhaylovich of Russia felt doubly blessed: Not only was his young wife, Natalya Naryshkina, pretty and devoted, but she had also just given him a son — Peter. Alexis had feared that the child might be like his sons from his first marriage, to Mariya Miloslavskaya: Fyodor and Ivan were weak and sickly. But the new *czarevitch*, as the son of a czar was called, was not only big and healthy, he was lively, intelligent, extremely curious, and precocious, too: He walked at the age of seven months.

Czar Alexis had been married to Mariya Miloslavskaya for 21 years before she died while giving birth in 1669. Of their 13 children, 5 had been sons, but only Fyodor and Ivan remained. As the relatives of the *czaritza* (the czar's wife), the Miloslavsky clan had enjoyed a powerful status for so many years that they now bitterly resented being replaced by Natalya Naryshkina's family. They also feared that the frail Miloslavsky czarevitches might die before their father did. One Miloslavsky in particular worried about the situation—Alexis's ambitious 15-year-old daughter, Sophia.

In January 1676, fate unexpectedly intervened on her side. At an outdoor ceremony in the dead of the brutal Russian winter, Czar Alexis caught a chill. In less than two weeks he was dead. The grieving Natalya was left with Peter, who was not yet four, and his younger sister, Natalya. Fifteen-year-old Fyodor was proclaimed czar, and Sophia seized the opportunity to step into the inner circle. She began attending meetings of the council of *boyars* (Russian noblemen) and participated in policy discussions. And she reinforced her growing power by staying close to Fyodor.

Peter divided his time between his studies in the Kremlin (the massive royal citadel in Moscow) and excursions to his father's villa at Kolomenskoe, on the Moscow River. He enjoyed a peaceful boyhood until 1682, when Czar Fyodor suddenly died. A succession crisis loomed: Although Fyodor had married twice, he had left no sons. Which of the two remaining czarevitches should become czar? The obvious choice was the elder son, 16-year-old Ivan, but many feared that the afflicted youth, who was epileptic and nearly blind, would not be able to handle the duties required of him. Instead, some voiced support for Peter. Although he was only 10 years old, he was robust and irrepressible. The boyars could not agree and declared that the people should decide. The citizens of Moscow clamored for Peter, who presented a much more czarlike figure than the frail Ivan.

Nineteen-year-old Sophia was outraged that Ivan had been denied his rightful place and that the Naryshkin family might come to power again. She was afraid that if Peter became czar, she would be forced to give up the political role she had already assumed under Fyodor. But once again, fate was on her side. This time, the *streltsy* (the czar's royal guard and personal army) were the agents of fortune. Shortly after Fyodor's funeral, two riders galloped into the streltsy quarters shouting that the Naryshkins had killed the czarevitch Ivan. The enraged streltsy grabbed their pikes and battle-axes and headed for the Kremlin. Though terrified by the mob, Natalya brought Ivan and Peter to the top of the Red Staircase, which descended to Cathedral Square, to show the streltsy that the czarevitches were safe. A few

In the same degree that [Sophia Miloslavskaya's] stature is broad, short and coarse, her mind is shrewd, subtle, unprejudiced and full of policy. And though she has never read Machiavelli, nor learned anything about him, all his maxims come naturally to her.

—MARQUIS DE BÉTHUNE
French ambassador
to Poland

asked Ivan if he was truly the czarevitch, and the frightened boy stammered his identity. Peter stood at his mother's side, silent and watchful.

Confused and embarrassed by the mistake, the streltsy were just about to break up when Prince Mikhail Dolgoruky, the despised son of their commander, shouted that he would see them all beaten if they did not depart immediately. The streltsy had come to the palace looking for a fight, and Dolgoruky's threats were all the excuse they needed. They

Natalya Naryshkina and the two young czarevitches, Peter (standing straight) and Ivan (cowering), are menaced at the top of the Red Staircase at the Kremlin during the bloody revolt of the streltsy in 1682.

19

Impaled and beheaded victims of the streltsy rampage in Moscow. Following the anti-Naryshkin purge, Czarevitch Ivan's sister, Sophia Miloslavskaya, became regent.

surged up the stairs, grabbed Dolgoruky, and flung him onto the raised pikes of their comrades below. The streltsy then tore through the palace, hunting down members and friends of the Naryshkin family and anyone else they felt was a threat to them, to the royal Miloslavskys, to Russia. Natalya huddled in the hall with Ivan and Peter, afraid to move or speak.

The nightmare continued the following day. By now liquor had intensified the streltsy's thirst for blood, and they returned to the Kremlin to hunt down Natalya's ambitious brother Ivan Naryshkin, who had been attempting to increase his family's power at the expense of the Miloslavskys. The streltsy ransacked the royal apartments, murdering anyone who resisted, but Ivan remained well hidden. On the third day, the streltsy demanded that Natalya turn over her brother, or they could not vouch for the safety of anyone — including young Peter. Sophia, who had kept silent through all the turmoil, now demanded that Natalya give up her brother. Numb with shock and grief, Natalya could only think of saving her beloved Peter, and she sent for her brother. Weeping, she accompanied him to the chapel for final prayers, then turned him over to the streltsy. After days of torture, including repeated beatings and the breaking of his ankles and wrists, Ivan was hacked to pieces, and his remains were ground into the mud. With this gory finale, the streltsy seemed at last to have had their fill.

The shrewd Sophia quickly turned the revolt — which many suspected she had instigated in the first place — to her advantage. She urged the streltsy to demand that the two czarevitches share power and that Ivan, as the elder, take precedence. Natalya, shocked and grief stricken, put up no resistance. The two boys were crowned czars, and Sophia became regent. She gave a banquet for the streltsy as the "saviors" of the royal family; she herself served them vodka. Sophia would rule as regent for seven years.

As the anointed czars, Ivan and Peter were obliged to attend formal state ceremonies and religious processions in Moscow. But Peter much preferred his life in the country, at the modest royal hunting lodge at Preobrazhenskoe. Sophia had sent Natalya and Peter to the lodge, about three miles northeast of Moscow, where she kept them on a small allowance. In the country, Peter enjoyed an upbringing that he would not have had in Moscow. He still had his studies, but he also had time to play in the beautiful fields and forests of the Russian countryside. His favorite pastime was war games, and he had the space to hold spectacular battles. He also had his "soldiers": As the son of the czar, Peter had been assigned companions, boys his own age, from the time he was very young. Peter grew up with these boys, the scions of the oldest noble families in the land and the sons of the lesser nobility, and they became his friends.

Peter formed his companions into regiments and provided them with uniforms, flags, drums, and even weapons. At age 11, he was allowed to replace his wooden cannons with real ones from the armory. Peter insisted that his friends advance through the ranks by proving their ability, and he set the example. He started himself at the lowest position, drummer boy, and then, as he participated in mock battles and gained "experience," he promoted himself. His favorite rank was bombardier — he loved to fire the cannons. By 1686, with the help of foreign mercenaries from the German Suburb outside Moscow, Peter had established a virtual military academy of several hundred boys. He kept one regiment at Preobrazhenskoe, and when he ran out of room there, he had housing set up in the nearby village of Semyonovskoe. From these beginnings were to come the proud elite troops of the Russian Imperial Guard.

Peter had a tremendous curiosity, and he was constantly striving to expand his knowledge and experience. He was particularly interested in the mechanical arts, and when he wanted to learn something, he did not rest until he mastered it. When he was 12 years old, he ordered a carpenter's bench and learned to operate a lathe. He practiced working with wood, stone, and leather. He hammered out iron in a blacksmith's shop and learned how to set type for books. In 1687 he obtained a sextant, a device that measures distance. None of the Rus-

Pretender to the Russian throne Sophia Miloslavskaya enraged Peter when she circulated this portrait of herself wearing the crown of the czars. She was defeated in a power struggle with Peter in 1689.

sians knew how it worked, so Peter went to the German Suburb to find a foreigner who did. A Dutch merchant, Franz Timmerman, told the eager czar that he would have to know geometry before he could understand the instrument. So Peter at once began to study mathematics.

The next year, Franz Timmerman was present at an even more important discovery in Peter's life. While walking on the royal estate in the village of Ismailovo, Peter and Timmerman came across a decrepit boat in a storehouse. It was unlike any boat Peter had ever seen; it did not resemble the huge, flat river barges that plowed the Volga and Moscow rivers, nor was it like the small, simple craft the nobility used for their leisure sailing. When told by Timmerman that it was a Western sailboat and that it could sail against the current, Peter insisted on trying it. A Dutch carpenter was brought from the German Suburb to repair the boat and he taught Peter how to sail on the Yauza River. Peter was so excited that he took the boat out daily, and he soon yearned for deeper water.

One of the most important duties of a czar was to provide an heir. Peter was 16, old enough to be married. Natalya picked out a bride for him from a well-established family. Eudoxia Lopukhina was simple, quiet, obedient, and religious. In Natalya's eyes, she was the perfect traditional wife, but she would prove to be completely unsuited to the dynamo that was her husband. Within two years, Peter and Eudoxia had two sons. Only his first son, Alexis, survived.

In the meantime, Sophia's high-handed behavior had alienated much of Moscow. She had adopted the title of autocrat and had commissioned a portrait of herself wearing the 12th-century Cap of Monomakh, used to crown the czars. Rumors circulated that she planned to marry her lover, Prince Basil Golitsyn, and depose Ivan and Peter. Sophia was not worried by the rumors and the resentment. Her sickly brother was no threat, and as long as the streltsy backed her, she felt she had nothing to fear from Peter and his boy army. She was wrong.

In the summer of 1689 the contest of wills began. At Preobrazhenskoe, soon after midnight on August 28, Peter was abruptly roused from sleep by a servant shouting that the czar's life was in danger. Memories of the slaughter he had witnessed as a child haunted Peter, and when he heard that the streltsy were coming for him, he flew from his apartments clad only in his nightdress. He rode into the surrounding woods to wait for a servant to bring him clothes, and when he was dressed, he and a small group of companions galloped off to take shelter in the Troitskaya fortress-monastery, 45 miles northeast of Moscow.

Peter's flight turned out to have been triggered by a false alarm: Sophia had not ordered the streltsy to take him — they were still in their quarters in Moscow. But both Peter and Sophia realized that there was no turning back now — the boyars had begun to take sides, and the conflict developed a momentum of its own. Peter made the first move: He ordered the streltsy to report to him at the monastery. Sophia tried to coax the streltsy into supporting her, but most of the boyars and public opinion had turned against her, and the streltsy did not want to find themselves on the losing side in the showdown. Sophia threatened to execute any who deserted her. After several days, Peter issued his final command to the streltsy: Report to him or face death as traitors. The streltsy began streaming out of Moscow to join Peter at Troitskaya. Sophia had no choice but to surrender. Peter had won his first true battle.

Sophia's supporters were beaten, executed, or sent into exile. Sophia was confined to a convent, where she would live out the rest of her days in seclusion. Peter wrote to Ivan suggesting that they both reign. He waited until Sophia had been conducted to the convent before he entered Moscow. In October, at the age of 17, he greeted Ivan at the Cathedral of the Assumption and embraced him in triumph. Two czars now ruled Russia, but it was clear to the people which one of them was the stronger.

> *Our sister [Sophia] . . . by her own will alone has taken over the conduct of our government, contrary to our desire and that of the people, and you know how patient we have been. . . . Let us not permit [her] to share our title and to meddle in affairs that we two should administer together, between men.*
>
> —PETER THE GREAT
> to his half brother and
> co-czar Ivan

2
The Jolly Company

If Natalya and the boyars who had supported Peter against Sophia expected him to abandon his carefree life at Preobrazhenskoe to assume the duties of a czar, they were soon disappointed. Peter was content to let his mother and an advisory council conduct the daily governing of the realm. He was more interested in staging mock battles and discovering the world of the German Suburb.

Peter was fascinated by the foreign enclave. The magnificent brick houses that stood on the wide avenues proudly showed off styled gardens and elaborate fountains. They were so unlike the small, dark rooms and simple design of the Russian homes. To the impressionable young czar, not only were the houses full of light, the people were, too. It seemed to Peter that the foreigners truly enjoyed themselves. They gave banquets, dances, and masquerades. The women were not shut away in separate rooms like Russian women; instead, they sat at table with the men, taking part in conversation and

Peter and his friends . . . made fun of everything, ignoring tradition, popular feeling, and their own self-respect, in the same way that children imitate the words, actions, and facial expressions of adults.

—VASILI KLYUCHEVSKY
Russian historian

As a young man, Peter's rapid physical and intellectual growth, his warlike inclinations, and his contempt for much of traditional Russian culture alarmed his mother and many of the tutors and boyars who attended him.

25

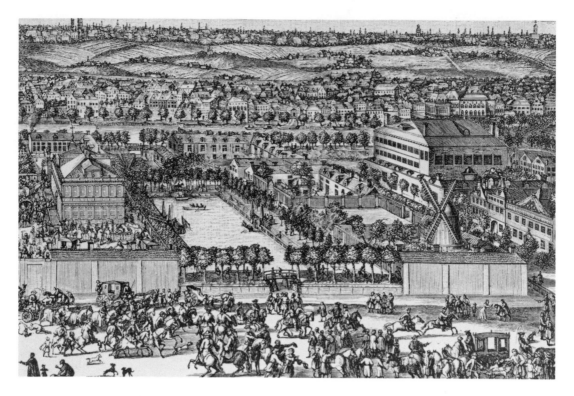

The German Suburb on the outskirts of Moscow, where Peter was introduced to the culture of Western Europe. The powerful Orthodox clergy in Moscow feared that the foreigners would corrupt the young czar.

even drinking with them. Peter had never been exposed to such lively, interesting women. He took a German mistress, a wine merchant's beautiful daughter named Anna Mons. Their affair would last 12 years, but Peter's love affair with Western culture would never end.

It was in the German Suburb that Peter met two men who also became very important to him. General Patrick Gordon was a 59-year-old Scottish Catholic who had served in the armies of several different European kings. The experience and technical knowledge of this soldier of fortune helped Peter forge his army. Gordon admired Peter's energy and drive, and he genuinely liked the czar. Peter looked to Gordon for military advice and fatherly encouragement. Peter's close friend and drinking companion from the German suburb was the Swiss adventurer François Lefort. The two met in 1690 and immediately struck up a friendship. Lefort was generous, fun loving, and mischievous. Also, he was the one person who could drink as much as Peter.

Best of all, he did not expect anything from Peter; he did not look to the czar to make him powerful or rich. Peter, accustomed to people seeking his favor, was very grateful for the genuine affection Lefort showed him.

Peter's comrades were not exclusively foreign. Some, such as Prince Mikhail Cherkassky, were elder statesmen from the oldest boyar families in Moscow. Still others were younger noblemen or men from middle-class backgrounds who found favor with Peter. Prince Fyodor Romadanovsky, whose father had been killed by the streltsy in 1682, shared with Peter a passionate hatred of that group, and he became one of the czar's most devoted subordinates. Aleksandr Menshikov, who had a lower-class background, was one of the boys assigned to Peter's circle at Preobrazhenskoe; he grew up with Peter and took part in his war games. Later he would become an indispensable aide and friend to the czar.

Scottish mercenary Patrick Gordon was a member of Peter's merry band of revelers. Gordon was to prove useful to Peter as a military adviser as well as a drinking companion.

François Lefort, one of Peter's favorite cronies during his early drinking days in Moscow. Peter liked the young adventurer from Geneva because he could "drink like a hero."

Together with his foreign and Russian friends, Peter founded the Jolly Company. Resembling a modern college fraternity, the Jolly Company enjoyed a boisterous camaraderie, played jokes and pranks, and indulged in a lot of feasting, drinking, brawling, and womanizing. The members hailed Bacchus, the Roman god of wine, as their patron. Wherever Peter went, up to 200 members of the Jolly Company might follow. The leading families of Moscow dreaded the sight of the czar coming to dinner or for a visit, knowing that the rowdy, raucous Jolly Company was not far behind. The company roamed from house to house, throwing parties, holding banquets, putting on fireworks displays, drinking prodigiously, and generally raising hell. During the winter, they rode around Moscow in sleighs, unexpectedly dropping in on people for drinks, which the disgruntled hosts were obliged to provide — no one dared refuse the czar service. Peter had an enormous, elegant house constructed for Lefort, which became the headquarters of the Jolly Company, with men and women of dubious reputation going in and out at all hours.

In addition to the Jolly Company, Peter established the All-Joking, All-Drunken Synod of Fools and Jesters. The mock synod was Peter's way of thumbing his nose at the Orthodox clergy, which, in Peter's view, wielded an all-too-pervasive — and stifling — influence over Russian society and government. At the head of the All-Drunken Synod was the "prince-pope," Peter's old tutor, Nikita Zotov. Others from the Jolly Company served as "cardinals," "bishops," and "deacons." Dressed in outlandish costumes, they held elaborate ceremonies, the purpose of which was to get abominably drunk.

Together with their "ecclesiastical" offices, Peter's followers were given "civil" titles taken from the positions they held in the mock battles at Preobrazhenskoe. King of Pressburg and king of Poland were the highest ranks. As he did on his battlefield, Peter placed himself in the lowest ranks; while serving the fake kings, princes, and popes, he laughingly called himself "your humble servant" or "your obedient slave." During his life, Peter would keep up this charade in which he and his closest officials switched roles.

Peter continued to drill his regiments at Preobrazhenskoe and to set up battles for his men to gain experience in war. His family and his subjects worried about his safety. In 1690 some gunpowder exploded and burned the czar's face; Peter just considered himself wounded in the line of duty. In the summer of 1691, Peter staged his largest battle ever, pitting the forces of the "king of Pressburg," Romadanovsky, against those of the "king of Poland," Ivan Buturlin. Prince Ivan Dolgoruky was mortally wounded and General Gordon was laid up in bed for a week with burns and a leg wound. Peter was delighted with the "performance" of his troops.

Along with Anna Mons, the German Suburb, and vodka, Peter had acquired another love — sailing. At Lake Pleshcheyevo, north of Moscow, he set up a workshop for Dutch shipwrights from the famous seaport of Zaandam. The czar alternated between working alongside the carpenters and practicing sailing on the lake. He invited his mother to come see his progress, but she was horrified that her son

I could not but adore the depth of the providence of God, that had raised up such a furious man to so absolute authority over so great a part of the world.

—GILBERT BURNET
bishop of Salisbury

Peter and a friend play chess at a typically raucous gathering in Moscow. Although Peter spent most of his teenage years carousing, he also managed to build and train a Russian army.

had taken up another activity that was so potentially dangerous. Peter longed to try sailing on the real sea, and in July 1693, after promising Natalya that he would not go out on the open ocean, he went to the only seaport Russia had — Arkhangel'sk, on the White Sea.

Arkhangel'sk was only 130 miles south of the Arctic Circle and frozen for half the year, but during the summer it was a noisy, active port. Ships unloaded goods from Europe, including cloth, wines, and other luxury items, and picked up the raw materials that Russia exported, such as hemp, furs, and grains. Peter boarded many of the ships to inspect the construction and talk to the crews. The ships' officers took Peter to the local taverns, where, over brandy, they talked about the great shipyards

of Holland and England. Peter loved the bustle of the docks and the smell of the salt air, and he jumped at the opportunity to sail his yacht, the *St. Peter*, into the White Sea as an escort for a merchant convoy. Thrilled by the pitch and roll of the ocean, Peter forgot about the promise he had made Natalya.

Peter felt that his mother did not fully understand him and chafed at the limits she placed on his behavior, but the bond between them was very strong, and Peter was desolate when she died that winter at the age of 42. Too depressed to attend the funeral, Peter went alone to her grave days later. Much of the affection and trust Peter had felt for his mother he now directed to his younger sister, Natalya, who was devoted to her brother and would remain so for her entire life.

His mother's death seemed to bring about a change in Peter's attitude. He began to think seriously about his responsibilities as czar and about the future of Russia. In the summer of 1694, Peter staged his last mock battle, a massive siege that lasted three weeks. But Peter had grown tired of playing at war; now he was ready for the real thing. Russia was still technically at war with the Turkish Ottoman Empire. Peter had been thinking about an assault on the Turkish fortifications on the Black Sea, in south Russia. For many years the Russian czars had wanted to establish control in south Russia, where the Turkish-supported Tatars looted villages and took Russian slaves at will. Peter had a second goal — a southern port from which to launch the navy he planned to build.

In 1695, Peter announced that the war with the Turk would resume that summer. His goal was to capture and hold the mouths of the Don and Dnieper rivers. Gordon, Lefort, and Fyodor Golovin were appointed commanders; Peter took the rank of bombardier. With a force of 31,000, including the Preobrazhenskoe and Semyonovskoe regiments, Peter

Peter (on horseback, with sword) and his new army assaulted the Turkish stronghold of Azov, on the Don River, during the summer of 1695. The Russians were repulsed, but a year later their second attack met with success.

set off in June 1695 to take the Turkish stronghold of Azov, on the Don. The regular Russian army, more than 100,000 strong, was sent to capture the fortresses on the Dnieper.

The siege of Azov lasted 14 weeks. Against the advice of Gordon, an impatient Peter twice attempted to storm the fortress, only to be repulsed. By autumn the Russians were low on food, supplies, and morale. Peter knew that he could not leave the men in the trenches during winter, and he reluctantly withdrew. The czar was humiliated and angry about the defeat; he was also sensitive to the criticism that his "foreign" troops — those he had trained in the Western military style — had failed, whereas the other, traditionally Russian troops had enjoyed some success on the Dnieper. Peter moved quickly to discover what had gone wrong and to try again. The problems of a split command and the lack of siege experience were easily corrected. Peter appointed a single commander, General Alexis Shein, to direct the army. He sent to Austria for experts in siege technology and strategy. But the most important problem Peter had encountered at

Peter's half brother, the weak and sickly Czar Ivan V, died in February 1696. Peter was left as Russia's absolute ruler, and he soon set about imposing his will on his country — and on Europe as well.

Azov would be more difficult to remedy. The Russians needed to be able to cut off Azov's supplies, which arrived by ship.

Peter needed a naval force, at once. The order went out to build 25 war galleys and hundreds of river barges — in 5 months. For the construction site Peter chose Voronezh, 300 miles south of Moscow on the Don River. Voronezh was surrounded by forests that would provide timber. Peter himself moved into a small house near the shipyard and labored each morning as a carpenter on a galley. Russian laborers and Dutch shipwrights toiled to meet the impossible schedule. Peter drove the enterprise relentlessly; even when he was away from Voronezh, he demanded reports on the progress of his fledgling navy.

In the middle of this feverish activity, in February 1696, Czar Ivan died. Although Ivan had done very little real governing, he had helped Peter by attending the formal functions of the office, leaving Peter free to pursue his own interests. Peter was grateful for that and grieved over the loss, but he regained his spirits as spring approached with its promise of a renewed campaign.

In May, Peter began the second Azov campaign. His army of 70,000 included Russians; Cossacks, fiercely independent mercenary soldiers from the Ukraine and south Russia; and Kalmucks, a warlike central Asian people who were superb horsemen. Peter appointed Lefort, despite his naval inexperience, admiral of the navy. At the mouth of the Don River, the Russian forces cut off Azov's supply ships. The assault on the fortress began, and after the Cossacks breached a wall, the Turks quickly surrendered. Peter allowed them to depart and the Russians occupied the fortress. Elated, he declared that he would build a settlement on the Sea of Azov, at a site the Cossacks called Taganrog.

Bolstered by his naval success, Peter decided to build a complete fleet at Voronezh. He issued a *ukase*, or edict, stipulating that everyone in the land must contribute: Each monastery and each great landowner was to provide the state with one ship. Those who failed to do so would lose their property. When a group of merchants from Moscow complained that 12 ships were too many for them to provide, Peter raised their quota to 14. The government would supply the timber; the rest of the materials, and the labor, would be provided by the Russian people. The building of the Southern Fleet was only the first of many enormously difficult projects the Russian people would be compelled to carry out in order to satisfy Peter's vision of a new Russia.

Peter and his troops celebrated the Azov victory with a triumphal procession through Moscow. Instead of displaying the traditional sacred icons, with their images of the Holy Mother or the Orthodox saints, Peter had erected what looked to the Muscovites like a pagan arch with images of Roman and Greek gods. The crowds lining the streets searched for the czar as the procession passed, looking for him inside the golden carriages or astride a white horse, leading his victorious troops. They were surprised to find Peter among a group of ship captains walking behind Lefort's elegant carriage. Dressed as a German seaman, in breeches and a short black coat, the czar of Russia walked the entire nine miles of the procession.

> *[Peter's] deliberate modesty in reality hid a deep sense of pride. True greatness scoffs at titles, clothes, and settings.*
>
> —HENRI TROYAT
> historian and Peter the
> Great biographer

3

The Great Embassy

With the military success at Azov under his belt, Peter now felt that he could stand as an equal with the European heads of state. He decided the time had come to expand his own education and to bring his nation to the attention of the rest of the world by visiting the Western countries. The czar began making plans for what would come to be known as the Great Embassy, an extended diplomatic tour of Europe.

It was an almost larger-than-life character that would be visiting the courts of the major European powers. At the outset of the Great Embassy, Peter was 24 years old. He was a giant of a man at six feet, eight inches tall, with long arms and enormous, powerful hands. His long legs and rapid stride meant that most of the time his companions had to run to keep up with him. With shoulder-length, wavy auburn hair, thin, stooped shoulders, piercing black eyes, and a mustache, the youthful Peter presented a striking figure. An involuntary twitching that sometimes afflicted his face, neck, and left arm — the symptoms of an undiagnosed ailment that would bother him throughout his life —

As a ruler, Peter knew neither moral nor political restraints, and lacked the most elementary political and social principles. His lack of judgment and his personal instability, combined with great talent and wide technical skill, astonished all foreigners who met Peter when he was 25.

—VASILI KLYUCHEVSKY
Russian historian

In March 1697, Peter and a company of almost 300 Russians embarked on the Great Embassy, an exhaustive, 18-month fact-finding tour of Europe. Among the countries visited by Peter were Sweden, Holland, Germany (East Prussia and the Electorate of Brandenburg), Austria, and England.

contributed to his unusual appearance. Along with his tremendous physique, Peter possessed tremendous energy. A couple hours of sleep each night was all he needed, and he was so restless that he did not sit still even for meals. Often he would eat a little, get up and go outside to walk around, then resume his meal. He had a voracious appetite and an insatiable intellect, and he devoured food and information with equal gusto. He was quick to laugh but even quicker to anger, capable of volcanic eruptions of ill temper. Those who provoked his wrath usually regretted it deeply.

The czar planned the embassy very carefully. Composed of more than 250 people, the delegation would include ambassadors and their staffs, secretaries, cooks, messengers, livery men, and even bears, jesters, and a multitude of dwarfs to provide entertainment. Peter intended to spend 18 months abroad. He knew that the idea of the czar leaving Russia for nearly two years would astonish and disturb his subjects. Never before had a Russian czar been absent from his lands for so long a time. His boyars and the Russian clergy feared that Peter, already enamored with Western ways, would become thoroughly corrupted and would abandon the Orthodox faith. But Peter was determined to go, and he would not be swayed from his plans.

If Peter's subjects were dismayed by the prospect of his absence, they were rather confused to discover that their six-foot, eight-inch czar planned to go incognito. Accompanying the Great Embassy were 35 "volunteers," who were to study the cities and the people of the West. Peter and Menshikov would be members of this group. The czar felt that by traveling in an unofficial capacity, he would avoid the tedious formal ceremonies and protocol he so hated and be free to explore as he pleased. At the same time he would try to observe how the Russian envoys were treated at the European courts; he was eager that the embassy be given the honor that he felt was due the official representatives of the czar of Russia. Peter gave instructions that no member of the embassy publicly address him as the czar, under penalty of death. For 18 months, he was to be known as Peter Mikhailov.

*He went across lands
and across seas,
He learned himself in
order to teach us;
He sought to converse
with czars
In order later to surprise
all of them.*

—GAVRIL DERZHAVIN
"To Peter the Great," 1776

Peter and the Great Embassy left Moscow on March 20, 1697. Their first stop was the Baltic port of Riga, in the Swedish territory of Livonia (modern Latvia). It was not an auspicious beginning: Much like the Jolly Company, the Russians arrived en masse, uninvited, and thirsty. The local governor was at a loss as to how to deal with a monarch who refused to be recognized; the Russian envoys were not even formally accredited to the Swedish court; and Peter's insistence on studying the city's fortifications made the Swedes nervous. (Livonia had once belonged to Russia.) Uncertain how to act, the governor treated the Russians according to protocol but provided no banquets or entertainment. Peter was incensed when the Swedes forced the Russians to pay for their own food and housing.

The other intended "hosts" to the embassy soon got word of the impending arrival of the uncouth Russian company and resolved to avoid Peter's wrath by staging grand receptions and state dinners for the czar's arrival. The Westerners were eager to meet the czar and the Russians, who were rumored

The Great Embassy arrives in Amsterdam, Holland. Many of the foreign courts that the embassy visited had never before received Russians, although tales of the occasionally loutish behavior of the guests preceded their arrival.

to be wild, exotic people dressed in long robes and tall hats like oriental potentates. Notwithstanding his "disguise," Peter was easily recognized, but his hosts played along with his desire to remain anonymous, although it seemed quite odd to them. Despite his efforts to remain unobtrusive, Peter was soon the central figure in a much-anticipated traveling circus.

From Riga, the embassy passed through the nearby duchy of Kurland, where Peter was lavishly entertained, to Brandenburg, the German state ruled by Elector Frederick III, who was eagerly awaiting Peter. Frederick wanted to make Brandenburg the center of a new kingdom, Prussia, and he hoped that the czar would help him. Frederick was eyeing the Swedish Baltic lands; he broached the subject of a joint Russian-Prussian campaign against the Swedes. But Peter was noncommittal; his interests still lay in south Russia.

The embassy stayed in Brandenburg longer than expected because Peter was awaiting the outcome of events in Poland, a Russian ally against the Turks. In 1696, the Polish king, John III Sobieski, had died, leaving a power vacuum. Louis XIV of France, an ally of the Turks, was attempting to put his own candidate on the empty throne. Peter would not tolerate a puppet of France on the Polish throne and threatened the Polish government: He would invade their country before permitting them to elect Louis's choice. The Poles promptly chose Augustus, elector of Saxony, a state in central Germany. Satisfied with this outcome, Peter and the embassy traveled on to the German electorate of Hanover, where two formidable ladies eagerly awaited his arrival.

Sophia, the widowed electress of Hanover, and her daughter, Sophia Charlotte, were excited by the opportunity to meet the czar. Sophia and her daughter were the first highborn European women Peter had ever met, and at first he was flustered by their scrutiny. Overcome with embarrassment, he put his face in his hands and stammered in German, "I cannot speak!" But Sophia and her daughter conversed with Peter until he began to feel more at ease. As soon as Peter relaxed, he became lively and talkative,

and his hostesses were delighted with his honesty and exuberance. Soon the Russians, Peter included, were gaily dancing with the ladies of the court. The event was recorded by Sophia Charlotte in her diary; she astutely observed that "[the czar] may have had no one to teach him how to eat properly, but he has a natural, unconstrained manner and a lively mind. He is at once very good and very bad. He is a perfect reflection of his country."

Next was Holland. Peter and Menshikov hurried on ahead of the embassy and arrived in August. Peter rushed straight to the famous shipyards at Zaandam, of which he had heard so much from the Dutch carpenters in Russia. He planned to spend the winter there, studying under the master shipwrights. An excited, enthusiastic pupil, Peter bought a set of tools and the typical dress of a Dutch carpenter and reported for work at the shipyard early each morning. However, the news that the czar of Russia was working as a common laborer brought out the curious from miles around, and soon the "incognito" Peter could not leave his cabin without attracting a sizable crowd that gawked and pointed. The czar found the attention unbearable and at the end of a week, disgusted, he left for Amsterdam.

Upon his arrival in Holland, Peter went to work as a carpenter in the great shipyards of Zaandam. The czar much preferred laboring on the docks to participating in formal diplomatic ceremonies.

Peter was amazed by the Dutch capital, for it was unlike any city that he had seen. Amsterdam was the center of the thriving United Provinces of the Netherlands. Although it had a population of only 2 million, Holland was an enormously wealthy nation. From the many branches of its extensive colonial empire to the bustling ports of Amsterdam and Rotterdam came nearly all the goods in demand in Europe, including spices from the East Indies. Peter observed the Dutch in Amsterdam — wealthy, industrious, contented people. This was the type of society Peter wanted to form in Russia.

Peter met Burgomaster Nicholas Witsen, the leading city official, and told him of his difficulty in working in Zaandam. Witsen promptly arranged for the czar to enter the shipyard of the Dutch East India Company, a private firm where Peter could work unmolested. Menshikov would work with Peter; others in the embassy were assigned to learn trades, including rope and sail making, and to study seamanship. In the East India shipyard, Peter worked as a carpenter on a frigate, learning its construction from scratch. He lived in a one-room cabin, cooking his own meals and cleaning his own things. Each day, Master Peter, as his Dutch coworkers called him, happily joined the other carpenters at work in the yard.

In addition to his work at the shipyard, Peter investigated everything that caught his interest. He learned how to run a printing press and how to engrave metals. He visited museums, mills, and schools. He watched the activity on the loading docks, pestering the ship captains and the dockworkers with numerous questions. He talked with engineers, architects, and doctors. After watching a street dentist pull teeth, Peter demanded to know how to do it. Thereafter — to the horror of the other members of the embassy — he considered dentistry one of his most valuable skills and carried with him a bag of dental instruments. His companions soon wished he had never heard of dentistry, for he insisted on treating their toothaches, often pulling their teeth with such fervor that he extracted gum tissue as well. The czar also attended medical lectures at the renowned Theatrum Anatomicum, where he observed the dissection of a corpse. Peter, who was fascinated by the internal workings of the human body made visible by the operation, reportedly grew so peeved at his boyars, who were disgusted by the corpse, that he forced them to bite off some of the exposed muscle.

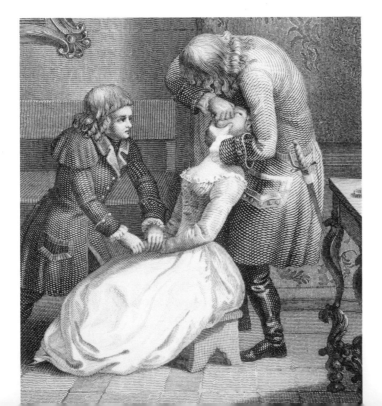

One of the many "skills" Peter learned during his travels was dentistry. Here, an unfortunate young woman has allowed the czar to extract one of her teeth.

Amsterdam was the favorite city of the sea-loving Peter during the Great Embassy. The czar would use Amsterdam as the model for his own city of St. Petersburg, founded in 1703.

Peter talked to the renowned, including Antonie van Leeuwenhoek, the inventor of the microscope, as well as to ordinary people. In shops, he conversed with bakers, dressmakers, and cobblers. In the streets he watched jugglers and artists. Whenever he came across someone with a valuable skill, he invited him to Russia to live among his people and teach them. Over beer at the local taverns, Peter questioned workers about life in Holland. He was determined to learn what made Holland so prosperous. One reason was trade: It had resulted in great riches for Holland. Russia, Peter noted to himself, had vast natural resources that could be traded in Europe. Another reason was that the Dutch were well educated, and Peter decided that schooling was of the utmost importance. Finally, Peter observed the religious atmosphere of Holland. The Dutch were very tolerant of other religions. No one faith dominated the country, and many different religions coexisted peacefully in the republic. Peter con-

cluded that the Russians would have to break free of the all-encompassing influence of the Orthodox church. It was the conservative church that had reinforced the Russians' xenophobia, their slavish obedience to tradition, and their lack of social and intellectual progress.

While the embassy was formally received by the Dutch parliament, Peter took advantage of an opportunity to meet with the stadtholder, the head of the republic. It was fortunate for Peter that William of Orange was in Holland, for William had to divide his time: He was also king of England. Peter had long admired William for his military exploits. The 47-year-old William, short and dour, was a bit daunted by the robust, energetic, and often crude Russian giant, but the 2 men soon developed a mutual respect. William invited Peter to England, assuring him that his anonymity would be preserved, and provided him with a ship to sail across the English Channel.

William III (pictured here at the Battle of the Boyne, July 1690), king of both England and Holland, was one of Peter's heroes. The czar was in awe of the Englishman's military exploits and hoped to equal them himself one day.

As in Amsterdam, Peter was interested in seeing everything in England that would give him insight into improving Russian society. Peter had an open invitation to the royal residences at Kensington and Windsor, but the czar, indifferent to the splendid settings and uninterested in formal state visits, spent little time at the castles. He preferred to wander the London streets, observing and questioning the locals. Peter had planned to stay in England only a couple of weeks. Four months later he reluctantly agreed to rejoin the embassy, which had remained in Holland in order to negotiate an alliance with William. The attempt to talk the Dutch into a treaty had failed utterly, however — William was more concerned about Louis XIV's territorial ambitions than about the Turks. Peter now turned his attention to Vienna, where Holy Roman Emperor Leopold I was about to conclude a peace with the Turks. The Russians hoped to arrive in time to prevent Leopold from weakening their claim to Azov.

The czar found Vienna, landlocked as it was, less stimulating than seafaring Holland or England. Leopold I was the conservative ruler of a staunchly Catholic realm. The Austrian court followed strict protocol and held stiffly formal ceremonies, behavior that exasperated Peter. The Viennese officials, for their part, were flustered by the idea of welcoming a monarch who would not be recognized. However, the visit did not go too badly. The Austrians found Peter to be modest and pleasant, albeit a bit impetuous and earthy for their tastes. And Peter was delighted to see the emperor forgo the usual state banquet for one of the famous Viennese masked balls. Dressed as a peasant, Peter danced deep into the night.

The czar also succeeded in achieving his strategic objective in Austria — ensuring that Russia did not lose Azov in the Austro-Turkish peace. By mid-July the embassy was ready to depart for Venice, and Peter went to take his farewell of Leopold. Suddenly, to the astonishment of the emperor and his court, Peter, Lefort, and Golovin leapt onto their horses and galloped furiously out of the city — in the opposite direction from Venice.

Peter had received a letter from Romadanovsky, who had remained in Moscow: The streltsy had revolted and were marching on the Kremlin. The fateful news had taken a month to reach the czar, and he feared that the streltsy had already succeeded in restoring Sophia to the throne. All of Peter's deep-seated hatred and fear of the streltsy boiled over. Determined to get back to Russia as quickly as possible, he rode day and night at breakneck speed, stopping only to eat and mount a fresh horse. Riding alongside Peter, Golovin and Lefort knew from the czar's grim manner that this time there would be a bloodbath.

He is a man of very hot temper, soon inflamed, and very brutal in his passion; he raises his natural heat by drinking much brandy.

—GILBERT BURNET
bishop of Salisbury

4

Mistress of the North

Peter was on his way across Poland when he received word that the streltsy's revolt had been quelled by Gordon, Shein, and Romadanovsky. Some of the rebel leaders had been imprisoned and a few executed, so there was no need for the czar's immediate return. Peter used the reprieve to remain in Poland, where he struck a military alliance with King Augustus. He did not forget about the streltsy, however; he had already decided that they would never again challenge the security of his reign. He arrived back in Moscow in the fall of 1698; it was not long before the purge began, and soon all Moscow was cowering before Peter's monumental rage.

The czar was convinced that there had been a plot to oust, and maybe even to kill, him. He was equally certain that Sophia had in some way been responsible. He wanted proof. He wanted to know who had instigated the revolt, what their aims had been, and how widespread the betrayal was. Fourteen secret chambers were built in and around Moscow, and they became the scene of shocking brutality. The interrogation of the streltsy was relentless in its cruelty. Day after day they were rounded up and hauled into Peter's torture chambers. They were beaten

[Peter] did not enjoy seeing people tortured—he did not, for instance, set bears on people merely to see what would happen, as Ivan the Terrible had done. He tortured for practical reasons of state: to extract information. He executed as punishment for treason. To him these were natural, traditional and even moral actions.

—ROBERT K. MASSIE
Peter the Great biographer

Peter, on the left, confronts an officer of the streltsy. The czar had received word of another streltsy uprising while still abroad; when he returned to Moscow, the members of the streltsy felt the full brunt of his anger.

with thick rods and flayed with the knout, a hard leather whip. Bones were broken and joints dislocated, skin was stripped from lacerated backs, and raw wounds were seared with red-hot irons or roasted over open flames. The chambers were filled with screaming and the stench of burning flesh. For hours on end the streltsy were harangued and tortured, until they lapsed into unconsciousness — only to be revived and tortured again.

Peter insisted that all of his closest companions take part in the mutilations: Romadanovsky, Lefort, Menshikov, Dolgoruky, Shein, and even his old tutor, Zotov. The czar viewed their participation as a test of loyalty. And given his preference to take a hands-on approach to a problem, it is very likely that Peter played some kind of personal role in the interrogations. He probably demanded answers of the men himself; there were even reports that he joined in the actual torture, wielding a knout or branding iron.

The net of suspicion had been cast over the general population. Priests who prayed for the victims were taken in; people on the street overheard to make a sympathetic comment about the streltsy were arrested. Even relatives of the accused found themselves in the torture chambers. Church officials appealed to Peter to halt the terror. The czar angrily told the clerics to stop meddling in state affairs, and the religious men no doubt held their tongue—no one was safe from Peter's vengeance.

Peter did not get any proof of a widespread conspiracy — he questioned Sophia personally and she denied any role — but the executions began nevertheless. (Sophia escaped the gallows, but Peter had her head shaved and forced her to take a nun's vows.) On October 10, the first of the beheadings and hangings took place. Ghastly cartloads of broken and mutilated men were pulled through the streets to the special gallows that had been erected throughout Moscow. Like gruesome Christmas decorations, the bodies were left to dangle throughout the winter, and the Muscovites went about their daily business with downcast eyes, to avoid the sight of so many corpses swinging in the wind.

Even if it is good and necessary, yet be it novel and our people will do nothing about it unless they are compelled.

—PETER THE GREAT
on the Russian resistance
to change

The czar himself attended the executions, seated on his horse, listening closely and watching with cold eyes. He wanted to make the connection very clear to the people of Russia: This was the result of betrayal and treason. Of the 2,000 men who had rebelled, 1,200 were executed. The sentences of the remainder were commuted. Some had their nose or ears lopped off; others were branded with hot iron and exiled. The streltsy's relatives were expelled from Moscow. The following spring, Peter formally dissolved the streltsy, thereby eliminating the only real internal threat to his power. Peter's savage treatment of the streltsy served him doubly: Not only did it demonstrate that he would tolerate no disloyalty, it also made it much easier for him to effect change in Russia. Despite much grumbling over Peter's new edicts, no one dared openly defy the czar.

And now the changes started. Peter began carrying a razor with him; whenever he encountered a boyar, out came the razor and off came the astonished boyar's beard. At the many celebrations held in honor of his return, Peter gleefully drew out the razor as soon as a bearded boyar came into view.

Broken by torture, the streltsy are paraded through the streets of Moscow in carts while Peter (mounted, on the right) looks on without compassion.

The westernization of Russia began after Peter returned from the Great Embassy. Beards and caftans were the first Russian traditions to fall prey to Peter's cultural purge.

The czar was delighted to begin the first of a long list of changes he had in mind for his country and his people, but the boyars were less than enthusiastic. To the Orthodox Russians, the beard was a symbol of a special bond with God. The Lord had made man in his image. Jesus had been bearded, thus to shave was tantamount to blasphemy. But Peter, after living among the western Europeans, felt that the long, unkempt beards of his boyars made them look barbaric and backward. Knowing that beards would now put them in disfavor — and hearing tales of how Peter, enraged by the boyars' obstinacy, would pull out beards by the roots — the boyars shaved. Soon the czar decreed that everyone except the clergy and the peasants were to shave off their beard. Those who wanted to keep their beard were required to pay a beard tax. Thus began the westernization of Russia.

Peter introduced more reforms. He began wielding a large pair of shears as well as a razor. At a dinner at Lefort's home, the czar clipped off the long, draped sleeves of his companions' clothes. Declaring that the traditional embroidered caftans, the brightly colored boots with turned-up toes, and the high fur hats of the Russian nobility interfered with movement and looked Oriental, Peter ordered that new clothing be worn. His court, all boyars, and government officials had to adopt German-style clothes: breeches, stockings, waistcoats, and shoes.

Noblewomen, too, were to dress like their counterparts in western Europe. Only the peasants were allowed to keep their traditional dress — long linen shirts tied at the waist, linen trousers, and felt or bark boots. Forcing change on the masses of uneducated peasants was beyond Peter's immediate capability.

One after another the changes came. Peter reformed the Russian coinage, standardizing the denominations of copper, silver, and gold kopecks. To raise state revenue, he decreed that all official documents be drawn up on stamped paper sold only by the government. Inspired by English practice, Peter introduced the Julian calendar. There were changes of a more personal nature as well, although some of them were unwelcome to Peter. His two closest friends, Lefort and Patrick Gordon, passed away. And the czar was determined to be rid of Eudoxia. She represented the past, and Peter had no patience for his passive, clinging wife. Eudoxia was forcibly packed off to a convent, where her head was shaved and she was given a new name. Alexis, Peter's son, was put under the care of Peter's sister, Natalya.

Russian boyars are accosted outside Moscow and subjected to Peter's beard census. The man on the right is having his beard clipped off; the man on the left has refused to part with his and must pay a beard tax.

Peter banished much that was traditionally Russian from Moscow, including his wife Eudoxia, who was confined to a convent. She accepted the trappings but not the vows of a nun and soon took her guard as a lover.

Peter's military plans were undergoing profound changes as well. Access to the Black Sea was no longer the key to the czar's strategy. Although the Southern Fleet was finished — 86 warships and over 500 supply barges had been built — the Great Embassy had failed to win support for a campaign against the Turks. Knowing that Russia alone could not defeat the Ottoman Empire, Peter neutralized the Turks as a primary threat by signing a treaty with them. Peter agreed to return the lower Dnieper to the Turks and to give up any claim to the Black Sea; but he had not abandoned his dream of ocean access, he had just changed direction. Shortly before he had returned to Moscow, during his talks with King Augustus, Peter had decided on a closer target, the Baltic Sea. Control of the Baltic would give Russia a warm-water port and access to the Atlantic. But to realize this objective, Peter would have to wrest the eastern Baltic coast from a power that was at least as formidable as the Turks. The czar began planning for a military campaign against the nation whose vast northern empire had won it the epithet Mistress of the North—Sweden.

Sweden was at the height of its imperial power. From Stockholm, a bustling seaport, the Swedes ruled the northern coast of the Baltic, most of the Baltic islands, all of Finland, and the provinces that surrounded the Gulf of Finland — Karelia, Ingria, Estonia, and Livonia. Sweden also controlled several key north German ports, including Stettin and Bremen, which gave the Swedes easy access to the Continent. And Swedish domination of the mouths of the major rivers that flowed into the Baltic, including the Oder, Weser, and Elbe of central Europe, and the Neva and Dvina rivers of the eastern Baltic, gave them a trade monopoly on goods to and from the Russian and central European interiors. Moreover, the Swedish army was one of the best in Europe.

Sweden and Russia had been traditional enemies since the 13th century, when Sweden first conquered Karelia and Ingria. Peter's own father had mounted an unsuccessful attack to retake the Neva, so Peter felt historically justified in eyeing the coast-

lands, even though they were settled not by Orthodox Russians, but primarily by Protestant
Germans. The czar was optimistic about a Baltic
campaign. Along with Poland, he had secured an
alliance with Denmark, another Baltic competitor
of Sweden's. And Sweden seemed to be vulnerable,
for in 1699 the Swedes crowned a new king — a 15-
year-old boy, Charles XII. But Peter was badly mis-
taken in perceiving Charles as a weak link. In reality, Charles of Sweden would prove to be a
remarkable ruler and the czar's perennial arch-
nemesis.

Charles was a born warrior. Tall and slender, with
fair skin, blue eyes, and a face deeply scarred by
smallpox, he was fascinated with military history,
and by the age of 15 he had mastered the science
of war. He loved danger and always tested the limits
of his own courage and prowess. He was an excellent
horseman and a skilled hunter. To harden himself
he slept on bare floors. He rode horses up steep cliffs
and hunted bears with only a wooden pitchfork. In
1700, when he learned that King Augustus of Poland had invaded Livonia, Charles quietly re-
marked, "We will make King Augustus go back the
way he came." A few weeks later, King Frederick of
Denmark invaded the Swedish territory of Holstein-
Gottorp. Peter was waiting for confirmation of peace
with the Ottomans before taking his part in the
three-pronged offensive against Sweden. The three
allies respected Sweden's military might but felt
Charles would not be able to handle them all. But
the army Charles commanded was one of the finest
in Europe, renowned for its mobility and discipline.
They carried the most advanced weapons of the
time, flintlock muskets and bayonets. The Russian
army still used the more cumbersome matchlock
guns.

On April 13, 1700, Charles set out for Denmark,
his first target. His strategy was to deal first with
one enemy, no matter what the others were doing
at the time, then to face the next. He did not want
to be drawn into fighting more than one at a time.
Charles quickly set up a siege of the Danish capital,
Copenhagen, and in two weeks the Danes surren-

> *I have resolved never to begin
> an unjust war, but also never
> to end a just war without
> overcoming my enemy.*
>
> —CHARLES XII
> king of Sweden

Charles XII (mounted at left) reviews his troops after the Battle of Narva, November 30, 1700. Peter was given a bitter taste of Charles's military genius at Narva, where the Swedes, outnumbered four to one, routed the Russians.

dered. Charles then set about securing Denmark while he prepared to transport his troops to the Baltic coast, where he expected to face Augustus, who was besieging Riga.

Peter was eagerly anticipating military action against Sweden, but his hands were tied until the peace with the Turks was finalized. In August he received word that the treaty had been signed, and he immediately declared war against Sweden, his stated aims being the recovery of Karelia and Livonia. But Peter's real objective during the Great Northern War, as the conflict between Sweden and Russia would come to be known, was access to the Baltic Sea, and thence the Atlantic. Peter would not relinquish the vision of a powerful Russian navy plying ocean waters, and it drew him, and his country, into a war that lasted 21 years.

Peter mobilized his army for an assault against the Ingrian coastal town of Narva. The siege works took more than a month to complete, and the Russian attack did not begin until early November. Augustus had already withdrawn from the siege of Riga to establish his winter camp. Shortly after Peter heard the report of Augustus's withdrawal, he learned that Charles and his army had landed just 150 miles south of Narva. The Swedish army had just completed a grueling march; Peter expected Charles to set up winter camp and rest his troops before resuming in the spring. On the evening of November 17, Peter left his army at Narva and went to Novgorod to check on supplies and reinforcements. On November 20, at daybreak, the Russians were taken completely by surprise when a detachment from the main Swedish force attacked, seemingly out of nowhere. The Russian lines, spread out over four miles, were panicked by the sudden assault and confused by a blinding snowstorm. The duc de Croy, the foreign commander in charge, was utterly unable to control the Russian soldiers. After sustaining heavy losses, the duc de Croy surrendered to Charles. A Swedish force of 10,000 had handily overcome 40,000 Russians.

Many years of intense hardship now began for the Russians. Peter realized that if he was to compete with the Swedes he would need an inexhaustible supply of well-trained troops, and he promptly announced new conscription terms of 25 years. To the Russian peasantry, who would bear the brunt of the war — as always — conscription into the army was an unhappy fate. Separated from their families, often never seeing their homes again, exposed to travel over harsh terrain, miserable weather, and constant warfare, the Russian soldiers carried a bitter burden. Nor did civilians escape the hardships brought about by the militarization of Russia. Women and children were put to work erecting fortifications around the cities. Tax money paid for the soldiers' new uniforms and weapons. Through the long years of war with Sweden, Peter would impose increasingly heavy levies on an already overtaxed populace.

In the spring of 1702, after leaving behind part of the army to continue the struggle in Livonia, Charles invaded Poland. He planned on making quick work of Augustus, but his campaign would last six years. Although his generals urged him to end the long Polish conflict, Charles refused to until he had completely subdued Augustus. Peter used the time to full advantage. He continued to improve

That we lived through this disaster . . . forced us to be industrious, laborious and experienced.

—PETER THE GREAT
on the Russian
loss at Narva

his army, and Russian troops began to win minor engagements. The czar also began to harass the Swedish ships on huge Lake Ladoga, using small boats built along its shores. Despite the defeat at Narva, Peter was determined to gain a foothold on the Baltic.

In August 1702 the Russians captured the Swedish fortress of Noteborg, situated at the crucial juncture where Lake Ladoga empties into the Neva River. Control of Noteborg meant control of the inland river network, and its loss meant that both the Neva and the province of Ingria lay open to a Russian advance. It was the first major victory for Peter's troops, and in a play on the site's Russian name of Oreshka (hazelnut), he wrote to Moscow jubilantly: "In truth, this nut was very hard, but, thank God, it has been happily cracked." Soon after, Peter retook the towns of Dorpat and Narva and began to erect huts and forts along the Neva riverbanks, on the several islands in the river, and along the coast. He called the new settlement St. Petersburg (now Leningrad). A steady stream of victories followed. They were small triumphs, but taken together they allowed Peter to press ever closer to the Baltic coast.

The defense of Noteborg. Peter's forces won their first important battle against the Swedes when they captured Noteborg, on Lake Ladoga, in August 1702.

In 1702, Peter took as his mistress 19-year-old Martha Skavronskaya, a Livonian peasant girl who would eventually become Catherine I, empress of Russia.

At this time a person came into Peter's life who would prove to be as important to him as any of his male friends, including Menshikov, who had become, since the death of Lefort and Gordon, Peter's closest companion. Indeed, it was Menshikov who was responsible for the new relationship. In his favorite's Moscow home, in the fall of 1703, Peter met a young peasant girl Menshikov had brought back from Livonia with him. Her original name was Martha Skavronskaya, but she had converted to Orthodoxy and taken the name Catherine. She had a full figure, dark eyes, and thick blond hair that she would later dye black to make her skin appear more fashionably white. It is likely that she was Menshikov's lover, but he cheerfully turned her over to Peter, who took an instant liking to the fun-loving, hardy, good-natured girl. The czar was 31; Catherine was 19. They would endure many tests and hardships together, but their affection for each other was unshakable. The illiterate Livonian peasant girl would become Peter's lover, his wife, the proclaimed czaritza, and, finally, empress of Russia.

5
The Power of Muscovy

Peter did not let military matters divert him from his program for domestic reform, and changes in Russia continued apace. Russian women were given more social freedom, and marriages arranged without the consent of both parties were forbidden. The traditional, formal obeisance to the czar, an embarrassing, overly deferential ritual in which his subjects dropped to their knees or prostrated themselves on the ground before him, was eliminated. In 1703, Peter founded the first Russian newspaper, *Vedomosti* (News), which contained not only news from abroad but also instructions on how to behave in polite society. The czar established several schools, including the School of Mathematics and Navigation and the School of Ancient and Modern Languages. And to increase the availability of books, especially technical manuals, Peter encouraged the manufacture of printing presses.

Peter was a kind man but a ruthless tsar [and] the surroundings in which he grew up were hardly likely to encourage in him any care for people's feelings or circumstances.

—VASILI KLYUCHEVSKY
Russian historian

Peter's energy, vision, and ruthlessness knew no bounds, and the first decade of the 18th century was the czar's most productive period. But for thousands of Russians pressed into service as soldiers or laborers, it was a time of misery and hardship.

61

Not all of Peter's changes were benevolent or constructive. In 1702 the czar had established the Secret Office, which would monitor the citizens of Russia for signs of discontent or treason. Heading the Secret Office was the merciless Romadanovsky. In the long tradition of Russian secret-police agencies, Romadanovsky's Secret Office used spying and eavesdropping, encouraged denunciations and betrayals, extracted information through torture, and became a feared and hated institution within Russia.

Peter had become a force of almost demonic energy and ambition. His vision of a new Russia drove him relentlessly, and so he drove the Russian people. The czar seemed to be everywhere at once during these years, crisscrossing his land countless times; directing construction in his new city, St. Petersburg; restructuring the government in Moscow; inspecting the shipbuilding at Voronezh; drilling soldiers at Preobrazhenskoe; always encouraging, urging, threatening, ordering, planning. All of Russia felt Peter's influence more and more directly. Those whose position in society or whose location far from Moscow had previously buffeted them from Peter's will now found that neither status nor distance softened the impact of the czar's manic activity.

In 1708 the czar, in his constant search for more revenue, founded a board of "fiscals," whose job was to come up with new ways to tax the population and to enforce tax collection. Every conceivable commodity was taxed. Tallow for candles, wheat for bread, and equipment for horses were taxed, as was all manner of food, including nuts, cucumbers, and melons. Russians paid taxes on their hats, boots, and beards, on baths, beds, and chimneys. Not only materials, but the various stages of life itself — births, marriages, and funerals — were taxed. Boyars, government officials, merchants, craftsmen, peasants — everyone paid. As quickly as it could be collected, the revenue was spent: on the construction of St. Petersburg, the building of foundries and factories, the expansion of the navy, and, especially, on the war with Sweden. At one point in Peter's

> *I am wedded to my army, in good times as in bad, for life and for death.*
>
> —CHARLES XII
> king of Sweden

reign, more than 90 percent of state resources was spent on the war.

For more revenue, Peter established numerous state monopolies that charged exorbitant prices for such items as coffins, tar, alcohol, and furs. Entertainment cost the Russians dearly: The sale of dice, chess pieces, and cards was controlled by the state. The most profitable monopoly was salt, which brought the government double the amount it cost to produce. Equally burdensome were the czar's draft laws. Peter had no qualms about exploiting his country's most valuable resource — the Russians themselves. Between 1704 and 1709, he drafted more than 300,000 men into the army. In addition, thousands of peasant laborers were ordered from their homes and farms to St. Petersburg, Voronezh, Azov, and Taganrog to work on construction projects. Conditions were deplorable, and like the slaves who toiled to build the great Pyramids for the Egyptian pharaohs, the Russian laborers died by the thousands. Whenever they found the opportunity, the workers fled; the military was also plagued by desertion. Peter simply filled the vacancies with other Russians.

Peter and his architects examine the blueprint for the czar's city on the Gulf of Finland — St. Petersburg. So many Russians died during the construction of the city that it became known as the "city built on bones."

Peter attempts to interrogate a Cossack. Unpredictable, warlike, and rebellious, the Cossacks were a perennial thorn in the czar's side. They engaged in frequent uprisings against Moscow and occasionally allied themselves with Peter's enemies.

Inevitably, resistance to the czar's programs sprang up. Between 1705 and 1708, the czar faced three serious rebellions in the south. The first and last of these were quickly put down, but in 1707, at a time when he was fully engaged with the Swedish army, Peter faced a much graver threat — the revolt of the Don Cossacks. The Cossacks lived throughout the Ukraine and along the Dnieper and Don rivers. Nomadic and warlike, the three main bands of Cossacks, the Ukrainian, the Don, and the Zaporozh'ye, traditionally offered refuge to army deserters, runaway serfs, political dissenters, and any other outcasts or refugees. They elected a leader, called an *ataman* (or *hetman* by the Ukrainian Cossacks), and lived by their own laws. Expert horsemen, Cossack mercenary cavalry bands at times allied with, at times fought against, Moscow. By Peter's time, many Cossacks, especially the Ukrainian, had settled in towns or on farms, but they continued to obey their own leaders.

In September 1707, in an attempt to retrieve army deserters who had fled to the Cossacks, Peter sent Prince Yuri Dolgoruky south with a military force. Kondraty Bulavin, the fierce ataman of Bakhmut, massacred Dolgoruky and his men and began a campaign to free the wretched workers at Azov, Taganrog, and Voronezh. By the following spring Bulavin and his band had attacked Azov and seriously threatened the upper Don. The czar sent Prince Vasily Dolgoruky, Yuri's brother, with a force of 10,000 infantry and dragoons, saying, "This rabble cannot be treated other than with cruelty."

Not until November 1708 did the czar's men succeed in quelling the revolt. Fearing Peter's wrath, the unpredictable Cossacks turned on Bulavin, hoping to capture him for the czar, and the ataman killed himself. At a final battle, 3,000 Cossacks died. Peter ordered hundreds of the surviving rebels hanged; their swinging corpses were displayed on rafts floated down the Don as a warning to those who would oppose the czar. The rebellion had unnerved the czar. At the height of Bulavin's rampage along the Don, Peter found himself facing a potentially disastrous situation: In June 1708, King Charles had invaded Russia. "The power of Muscovy," Charles declared as he launched his invasion, "must be broken and destroyed."

In August 1706, after deposing Augustus and installing King Stanislaw on the Polish throne, Charles had finally brought his Polish campaign to a successful conclusion. Peter knew that Charles would now turn on Russia. Charles, riding high on his victory, not only intended to retake every last piece of Swedish territory along the Baltic, he wanted to decisively defeat the Russians in battle and impose his own terms on Peter. The czar, he told his officers, "is not yet humiliated enough."

Peter began to prepare for the invasion. In January 1707 he ordered that a huge band of territory in eastern Poland, the ground over which Charles would advance, be burnt. This scorched-earth policy made it extremely difficult for an invading army to maintain adequate provisions. The czar ordered additional fortifications for Moscow and St. Peters-

> *Challenge brought out the steel [in Charles]—the streaks of hardness and ruthlessness in his character. . . . His officers and soldiers saw his self-discipline, his physical courage, his willingness not only to share but to exceed their own physical hardship. . . . They would attack wherever he pointed his sword: If he asked it, it could be done.*
>
> —ROBERT K. MASSIE
> on King Charles XII

Charles XII (left) greets King Stanislaw I of Poland. After defeating Poland's king Augustus in 1706, Charles placed Stanislaw on the throne.

burg, worked incessantly to train and equip the army, and pondered a defensive strategy. Peter was unwilling to risk his army in an open fight against Charles's rigorously trained, battle-hardened force. He and Menshikov decided on a largely defensive campaign. Menshikov's cavalry would shadow the Swedish army, harassing them with lightning strikes and then quickly withdrawing, while the bulk of the main Russian force would try and draw Charles into a vulnerable position.

These were trying times for Peter. Plagued by ill health, frustrated over the Bulavin revolt, and anxious over the Swedish approach, he turned for comfort to Catherine. His mistress had become his indispensable confidante and companion. As an acknowledgment of her importance to him and to reward her devotion and loyalty, Peter married her. Although his closest officials knew of the union, it was kept secret from the Russian people, who were not yet ready for a peasant czaritza.

After the marriage, Peter joined the main Russian army at Grodno, on the Lithuanian border about 150 miles northeast of Warsaw, to monitor the Swedish advance. Menshikov was doing his job well: The Russian cavalry laid waste to the land and harried the Swedish columns as they marched toward the Vistula River. Yet the Swedish advance was relentless, and Peter expected the Swedes to force a confrontation. But Charles did not want to engage the Russian army so far from his intended target — Moscow. He wanted to draw Peter into thinking he would march due east to meet the Russian army, when actually he intended to veer north in order to encircle the Russians and drive them toward Moscow.

The Swedes endured an arduous march through the bogs and marshes of northern Poland, dragging heavy artillery through mud and thick forests. They were exhausted but continued to follow their king's furious pace without question. They crossed the Vistula and Narew rivers to come within striking distance of Grodno. Charles did not know that Peter was with the Russian army at Grodno, or he might have launched a major assault right there. When Peter learned that the Swedish king was camped nearby, he ordered an attack, hoping to take Charles by surprise. The Russian offensive was quickly beaten back by the Swedish force, and Charles and his weary men finally stopped to set up winter camp.

With the coming of spring, Peter watched expectantly to see what Charles would do. The Swedes could move north against St. Petersburg or east to Moscow or even carry out a combination of both. In June, Charles broke camp and marched south. He forded the Berezina River 50 miles from Minsk, crossing into Russian territory and outflanking the Russian army. Immediately, Russian regiments were sent south, but their lines were spread too thin, and at the town of Golovchin the Swedes found a weak point and broke through. After four hours of heavy fighting, the Russians retreated. But Peter found praiseworthy elements to this engagement: His men had stood firm against a fierce attack, inflicted substantial losses on the Swedes, and retreated in an orderly fashion.

Peter's old friend Alexander Menshikov was put in charge of the Russian cavalry during the Swedish invasion. Menshikov's dragoons hounded the Swedes across the Ukraine and eventually trapped them at the Dnieper River in 1709.

Despite the Swedish victory at Golovchin, Peter's space-for-time strategy was working, and Charles found himself in a rapidly disintegrating position. He was running dangerously low on supplies, and he needed replacements for the soldiers he had lost at Golovchin. His men were hungry, tired, and frustrated by the elusive tactics of the Russians. Menshikov's cavalry harassed Charles's men constantly; stragglers and strays on the edges of the Swedish lines were picked off by roving bands of Cossacks and Kalmucks. When the Swedes mustered for an attack, the enemy horsemen simply melted away into the vast Russian spaces.

Charles sent orders to General Adam Lewenhaupt in Riga to bring more men and provisions. Lewenhaupt did not move quickly enough, and Charles wasted two summer months before he decided he could wait no longer. Impatient and concerned for the welfare of his troops, he ordered his men to march farther south, where the Russian cavalry had not yet devastated the land. Charles had lost the momentum for a drive against Moscow, but he felt he would rebound quickly once Lewenhaupt arrived.

Charles never made the rendezvous with his general. Lewenhaupt's force, exhausted by the long, three-month march and weighed down by heavy baggage trains, could not outrace the Russian cavalry. In early October the Russians cut Lewenhaupt off from his destination and forced a stand at the village of Lesnaya, about 100 miles southwest of Smolensk. It was a disastrous defeat for the Swedes. After a day of savage fighting, the Swedish ranks fell apart. Two thousand Swedes died and 3,000 were taken prisoner. All the supplies Charles so desperately needed — food, clothing, ammunition, medicine — were captured by the Russians. Lewenhaupt and a small force escaped south to Charles and the main Swedish army. Upon seeing the pitiful remnants of Lewenhaupt's force — minus any provisions — Charles was deeply disappointed. Still, he remained optimistic, for he had just acquired an ally he hoped would turn the tide against Peter. Mazepa, the 63-year-old hetman of the Ukrainian Cossacks,

Mazepa, hetman of the Ukrainian Cossacks, allied his forces — to Peter's dismay — with the invading Swedes in 1708. Mazepa's army was destroyed by Menshikov at the Dnieper in June 1709.

had defected to the Swedes. The Cossacks wanted to remain independent of Moscow, and Mazepa distrusted the czar, who was becoming strong enough to impose his will on the Cossacks.

The news of Mazepa's betrayal was a severe blow to Peter. In early November, he ordered Menshikov's cavalry to make an example of the Cossack city of Baturin. The Cossacks responded to a show of force, and Peter wielded it cruelly to prevent Mazepa's action from inciting other Cossack bands to join Charles. Menshikov's men massacred everyone in Baturin, 7,000 in all, and razed the town. Charles would get no more Cossack support.

Now the cat-and-mouse game that would result in the destruction of the Swedish army began. An enraged and frustrated Charles, hoping to draw the main Russian army into a major, decisive battle, pursued Peter deep into the Russian interior. But the Russian army refused to fight and instead continued to withdraw. Charles would not give up the chase, and as the deadly Russian winter closed in around them, the Swedish king and his army found themselves in a nightmarish situation — ill equipped, shelterless, their food and water dwindling rapidly, and exposed to elements more merciless than any Russian army. While Peter's men bivouacked comfortably at well-supplied encampments, the Swedes froze to death by the thousands.

Charles got his wish for a fight the following spring, but his army had been irreparably weakened by the Russian winter, and they were routed by Peter's forces at the Battle of Poltava on June 28, 1709. On June 30, the Russian cavalry caught up with the remains of the retreating Swedish army. The Swedish troops were trapped. Having reached the Dnieper River, they could not all cross, because the Russians had burned most of the boats that had been assembled earlier by the Cossacks. Charles,

A victorious Peter (right, on white horse) surveys the field — including some captured Swedish soldiers (center) — after the Battle of Poltava, June 28, 1709.

faint from blood loss and shock brought on by a wound he suffered at Poltava, at first resisted his officers' pleas to save himself, but he finally allowed himself to be ferried across the river into the territory of the Tatar khan Devlet Gerey. About 900 of his men succeeded in crossing the river with him; Lewenhaupt agreed to stay with the troops on the other side to face the Russians. Mazepa escaped with Charles, but most of his men remained with Lewenhaupt.

On July 1, Menshikov and 8,000 Russian cavalry appeared on the heights above the river; the disheartened Swedes at once surrendered. Mazepa's fearless Cossacks would not surrender but instead fought to the last man, knowing that they would die at Menshikov's or Peter's hands in any event. Charles, on the other side of the river, could only stand by and watch bitterly. His magnificent army, the pride of the Baltic, had been broken.

Charles XII, wounded at Poltava, rests on the banks of the Dnieper and ponders his defeat while his aides attempt to convince him to cross the river to safety before the pursuing Russians arrive.

6

Window on the West

The defeat of mighty Sweden was the talk of every court in Europe, and the new power of Russia made monarchs from London to Vienna apprehensive. Peter reveled in his new stature. No longer was he looked upon as an unsophisticated marginal player in the world of European power politics. Now welcomed into Europe's diplomatic folds, Peter began to receive inquiries — even, astonishingly, from France's Louis XIV—about establishing alliances.

Well into the summer of 1709 the boisterous victory celebrations continued across Russia. In Moscow, pealing church bells and booming cannons delivered an endless paean. Peter rewarded all the officers involved in Poltava: Menshikov was promoted to field marshal; Sheremetev received a new estate. The czar even accepted promotions for himself, to lieutenant general and rear admiral.

With Swedish fortunes at their lowest point, Peter was determined to take all he could get. He ordered Sheremetev to occupy Riga, and he sent Menshikov

When our neighbors hear about what has happened, they will say: it was not into a foreign land that the army and power of Sweden ventured but some deep sea; they plunged in and disappeared like lead in water.

—FEOFAN PROVOPOVICH
Russian monk, on the
Russian victory at Poltava,
June 1709

The czar at the site of St. Petersburg, his city at the mouth of the Neva River. The construction of St. Petersburg was the project that was closest to Peter's heart, and following the defeat of the Swedes in 1709, he turned his full attention to its completion.

with the cavalry to Poland to help Augustus regain the crown after Charles's puppet king, Stanislaw, fled. In October, Peter met with Augustus to renew their alliance, and by the end of the month, Menshikov's force had driven the remaining Swedish troops from Poland. After his discussions with Augustus, Peter traveled to Prussia to secure an alliance with King Frederick I. Peter also arranged a marriage for Czarevitch Alexis before returning to Russia on December 12.

The betrothal of the czarevitch to a foreign princess was another radical departure from Muscovite tradition. To Peter it signified the improved status of his country; political marriages were common among the European royal houses, and now Russia appeared to be an acceptable, even a desirable, alliance. Alexis's intended bride was Charlotte of Wolfenbüttel. Charlotte was a quiet, tall, pockmarked 16 year old. She was not particularly happy about the prospect of spending her life in the uncivilized backwoods of Europe, but she was prepared to accept her fate.

By this time, there was little real closeness between the czar and his son. While he was growing up, Alexis had seen his father only on occasion, when the czar was in a mood to note his progress or wanted him at an official celebration. And nature could not have given Peter a son more alien in personality and temperament. Everything Peter was — energetic, impulsive, passionate, decisive — Alexis was not. The czarevitch was languid and reflective. He was better educated than his father, and his tastes were intellectual, running to quiet study and theological discussion. Deeply Orthodox, he was offended by Peter's disdain for the church. As much as Peter despised the rituals and traditions of old Moscow, his son loved them. Alexis was bored by politics, hated physical labor, and despised the military. The only trait he had in common with Peter was an ability to consume large amounts of alcohol. The czarevitch had formed his own band of drinking companions, men whose disaffection with the czar led them to Alexis, who, they hoped, would reverse Peter's reforms after the czar's death.

The mere sight of the Czar was enough to make the weak-willed boy's blood freeze in his veins. When his father kissed him, he was repelled by the masculine smell of tobacco, leather, and sweat that clung to the sovereign's clothing. He grew cunning, hypocritical, by turns amiable and surly, brutal and cowardly.

—HENRI TROYAT
on Czarevitch Alexis

Peter's son Alexis, in a portrait that belies his true nature. Unlike his father, Alexis had no military inclinations whatsoever; he would rather have studied theology than gone to war.

During the spring of 1710 Peter resumed military operations on the Baltic coast. He fell ill in May and could not campaign for a month, but in June his army captured Vyborg, giving the czar Karelia as a northern buffer to St. Petersburg. By midsummer, Peter had control of Karelia, Livonia, and Estonia, and he wrote: "The enemy does not now possess a single town on the left side of the Baltic." With Sweden neutralized for the time being, Peter turned his attention toward his pet project, the construction of his "paradise," St. Petersburg.

The first structures at St. Petersburg had been military forts and outposts — the Fortress of St. Peter and St. Paul began as a hut on a small island in the Neva. Simple wooden huts for housing soldiers and workers went up along the riverbanks, and despite his absence from the area and his preoccupation with the war, Peter ordered that construction in the city continue, and he always kept abreast of its progress. He took a keen personal interest in it and gave the architects detailed plans for gardens, parks, palaces, and government structures. In 1703, Peter had appointed the Italian architect Domenico Trezzini, who had built a palace for King Frederick of Denmark, as St. Petersburg's master architect. Trezzini's designs were in the baroque style of northern Europe, heavily influenced by Holland. Peter wanted to reproduce Amsterdam, complete with canals, at St. Petersburg.

Around the wooden structures, Trezzini began to build larger, grander edifices of brick and stone. There were no quarries in the swampy marshland along the Baltic coast, and getting enough stone became an enormous problem. Peter decreed that no stone was to be used anywhere in Russia except St. Petersburg, and he commanded that every vehicle that entered St. Petersburg bring in three paving stones for the roads. The city, which had begun on islands in the river, gradually spread out east, to the riverbanks and the mainland. Merchants moved in to establish lucrative supply shops. Virtually everything — food, clothing, building materials—had to be imported.

In 1704, Peter ordered each province to send 40,000 men to St. Petersburg. Some served a short period of time, others spent their life there. Because of its enormous cost in human lives, St. Petersburg became known as "a city built on bones." Thousands died, and everyone existed under the harshest conditions. Historian and Peter the Great biographer Henri Troyat described the deplorable state of the conscripts, who worked daily "from sunup to sundown, lodged in filthy huts, underfed, mistreated, [without] even the indispensable tools for their task. . . . To build up the low banks of the river, the wretched workers carried earth in the skirts of their garments or in sacks made from old matting. Often they labored in the middle of marshes, in water up to their waists. The knout was used for the least breach of discipline. If a man was caught attempting to flee, his nostrils were cut to the bone. The ragged throng that swarmed about the scaffolding was attacked by the elements, by scurvy, by dysentery. Every day corpses piled up in the common grave."

I intend to imitate Amsterdam in my city of St. Petersburg.

—PETER THE GREAT

Those who refused to work on such projects as St. Petersburg paid a heavy price. Forced labor was the fate of many common Russians during Peter's reign.

Peter found that he had to create more than just buildings to make St. Petersburg a true city: He had to give it life. His nobles were not especially keen on giving up their comfortable homes in Moscow and their provincial estates for the wet, distant Neva marshes, but Peter was typically unconcerned with anyone else's feelings. In 1708 he brought his own family, including his sister Natalya and his half sisters, to the new city and commanded hundreds of Moscow nobles and rich merchants to move there also. They had to erect houses at their own expense — the nobles on the left bank of the Neva, the merchants on the right. Strict rules were issued for the size, facade, and even internal furnishing of the houses, depending on the owner's status.

During the early years of St. Petersburg, the transplanted Muscovites found life dull, expensive, and even dangerous. Surrounded by swamp, St. Petersburg's citizens were forced to import food from Moscow and the south year-round. Merchants could charge exorbitant prices for goods both within the city and in the growing suburbs just outside it. Fire was a constant threat, and Peter organized a watch system to catch fires before they got out of control.

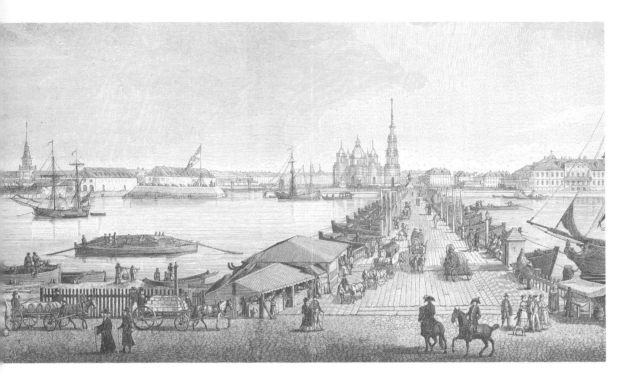

The maritime city of St. Petersburg. Originally only a small outpost on the point where the Neva River meets the Gulf of Finland, Peter transformed it into a cosmopolitan "Venice of the North."

Because the city was at sea level, flooding was a problem. When the winds were high or the Neva was swollen, bells tolled a warning to the people. In a 1706 letter to Menshikov, Peter described his rather boorish reaction to such occurrences: "Here it was entertaining to watch how the people, not only the peasants but their women, too, sat on the roofs and in trees during the flood."

Despite fire and flood, St. Petersburg, like everyone and everything else in Russia, yielded to the will of Peter, and gradually turned into the lovely city of pastel yellow and blue houses and charming canals that would earn it the nickname Venice of the North. The center of the new city was Trinity Square, on Petrograd Island. On the square stood the wooden Church of the Holy Trinity — where Peter attended services — the state chancellery, the government printing office, and the city's first hospital. Several of Peter's highest officials and closest friends had homes built along the square. And just off the square was the comfortable Four Frigates Tavern, often frequented by the czar himself.

Downstream lay Vasilevsky Island, the largest of the river islands. Peter had given most of the land there to Menshikov, who erected an elegant, three-story stone palace with a bright red, iron-plated roof. Menshikov's tastes were extravagant, and he furnished his house with rich brocaded tapestries and expensive imported furniture embellished in gold and silver. Because Peter did not like formal entertaining, grand celebrations took place at Menshikov's house, which boasted an enormous reception hall. The czar treated Menshikov's palace as his own, coming and going as he pleased.

The houses built in St. Petersburg for Peter and Catherine reflected their divergent tastes. Peter's Winter Palace was an undistinguished, two-story wooden building. In 1710, Trezzini began construction of the Summer Palace, on a site upriver. The 14-room palace, with its pale yellow walls and large windows on the water, was open, airy, and well suited to the summer heat. In Catherine's rooms were parquet floors, Chinese silk wallpaper, tables with inlaid mother-of-pearl or ivory, and tapestries.

The czar forced his people to build St. Petersburg, and once it was finished, he forced them to live there. In 1709, a large portion of Moscow's noble families were ordered to populate the new city — and to learn how to sail.

An idealized portrait of Peter's wife Catherine. After the czar's death, the task of preserving his reforms would fall to her rather than to a male heir.

Peter's sparsely furnished rooms were much simpler. The paneled walls of his study displayed blue Dutch tiles with nautical motifs or country scenes. His desk held a ship's clock and a compass. And of course, Peter set up a workroom. When he was at the palace he spent an hour or two every day working with his lathes in wood or ivory. He was very talented with his hands and proud of his ability. One of his finest products was completed in February 1712, when he presented a six-branched ivory and ebony chandelier to Catherine.

Through the early years of the Great Northern War, Catherine had remained at Peter's side. Calm, honest, and devoted, she was his friend and his staunchest supporter. By 1712, she had borne him five children. Peter had married her in a private ceremony in 1707; now he felt that Catherine deserved to be formally acclaimed as the czaritza. On February 19, 1712, Peter remarried Catherine in a ceremony held in Menshikov's private chapel, followed by a huge celebration that ended with a lavish dinner and fireworks.

In 1716, Peter replaced Trezzini with the French architect Alexandre Jean Baptiste LeBlond. LeBlond built the wide boulevard called Nevsky Prospekt, which quickly became the city's central avenue. Despite some underhanded resistance from Menshi-

On February 19, 1712, the czar remarried his wife Catherine in St. Petersburg. The wedding was followed by this massive banquet and a night-long celebration on the streets of the city.

kov, who resented the foreigner's influence and favor with Peter, LeBlond set up a system of canals on the east side of Vasilevsky Island. Peter especially liked the canals because they reminded him of Holland and provided an opportunity to get around by boat.

The czar also took an active interest in LeBlond's Summer Garden, located behind the Summer Palace. Peter himself selected the trees to line the avenues of the 37-acre retreat: chestnut, oak, elm, lime, and even fruit and cypress trees from the south. Flowers—tulips, lilacs, roses, and carnations

Peter engages in his beloved pastime — sailing on the Neva River. Among his passengers is his wife Catherine.

— added color and fragrance. Bushes were neatly trimmed into circles and cones. The garden contained a glass conservatory to grow citrus trees and displayed elegant Italian sculptures. Sparkling water splashed from 50 fountains. Peter decided that such a treasure should be open to the public, and the Summer Garden became a favorite spot for strolling or relaxing on warm summer evenings.

To the czar, the water was the most attractive part of St. Petersburg, and he wanted to maintain its importance in the capital. Although he allowed a small number of wooden bridges to be erected over some of the smaller streams, the czar forbade any across the Neva. To get from one shore to the other or to get from the mainland to any of the islands, 20 ferries were established. Much of the year, however, the ferries had trouble crossing the river because of ice. In winter, when the river froze, people simply walked or rode sleds across. In the autumn and spring the ice was not fully formed in places, making crossing by boat difficult, and on foot or sled dangerous. Peter solved the problem for himself by rigging up a boat on top of a sled so that he could glide or sail across depending on the river's condition.

Sailing was still the czar's passion. Peter knew that most of the new capital's populace did not share his passion, and he was intent on making his countrymen get over their dislike of boating. He ordered every noble to maintain his own boat and to attend classes on sailing. To curry favor with the czar, St. Petersburg's nobles gritted their teeth, donned their most elegant Western-style clothes, and spent their leisure time sailing. To escape the intolerable summer heat, Peter liked nothing better than to maneuver his yacht around the gulf, and one of his greatest pleasures was to look around and see members of St. Petersburg society skillfully — or not so skillfully — tacking their boats back and forth with him. He always eagerly awaited the coming of summer, when once again he could stand on the deck of a ship, feel the wind on his face and taste the salt of the sea, and gaze at his Window on the West, the magnificent city he had created from a swamp.

Gem of the Northern world, amazing, From gloomy wood and swamp upsprung, Had risen, in pride and splendour blazing.

—ALEKSANDR PUSHKIN
from "The Bronze Horseman," 1833

7

"My Own Unworthy Son"

Peter had not forgotten about his enemy Charles, and in April 1711, using the threat of his Southern Fleet, he tried to bully the Turkish sultan Ahmed, who had given the Swedish king political asylum, into giving up Charles, or at least expelling him from Ottoman territory. The sultan did not react well to the czar's threats — he declared war on Russia. With Poltava behind him, Peter was confident that he would quickly overcome the Turks, but he carelessly underestimated the size, strength, and speed of the Ottoman army. On a drive south through Moldavia (modern Romania), Peter and his army of 38,000 were caught by surprise at the Prut River and surrounded by 200,000 Turks. Faced with a shattering defeat and possible capture, Peter sued for peace. The czar had no choice but to accept harsh terms, including the surrender of Azov and Taganrog, the abandonment of any claim to the Black Sea, and unhindered passage for Charles back to Sweden.

You have carried your disobedience to the highest pitch by your flight and by putting yourself like a traitor under a foreign protection. . . . What wrong and what grief have you thereby occasioned to your father, and what shame have you drawn upon your own country!

—PETER THE GREAT
to his son Alexis,
October 1717

As they grew older, Peter and Catherine became increasingly concerned with the question of a male heir to the Russian throne. Alexis, Peter's son by his previous wife, Eudoxia, was the rightful heir, but he feuded constantly with his father and fell victim to Peter's rage and paranoia.

Charlotte of Wolfenbüttel, the German princess who married Peter's son Alexis in 1711. The unfortunate Charlotte was mistreated by Alexis, and she died, alone and unhappy, in 1715.

Peter was deeply embarrassed by the Prut fiasco, but he learned a valuable lesson about overconfidence. In the summers of 1713 and 1714, the Russian navy erased the depressing memory of the Prut campaign with a series of brilliant victories that captured most of the Baltic coast of Finland from the Swedes. The highlight of the Finnish campaign occurred in August 1714 at Cape Hangö, at the northwestern edge of the Gulf of Finland, where Russian galleys soundly defeated a Swedish force, capturing the fleet commander and his flagship. The Finnish campaign was one of Peter's most satisfying victories, sweeping the Swedish navy from the eastern Baltic and ensuring the safety of the czar's beloved St. Petersburg.

In October 1711, Peter had attended the wedding of Alexis and Charlotte of Wolfenbüttel in Torgau. While Alexis, on Peter's command, was reluctantly taking part in the initial Finnish campaign, Charlotte moved to St. Petersburg in the spring of 1713. She felt quite alone in the Russian city and was relieved when Alexis returned at the end of the summer. However, back among his cohorts, Alexis soon slipped into his old life of drinking and carousing, and he alternately ignored and abused his new wife. The marriage quickly disintegrated. When Charlotte had their first child, Natalya, in July 1714, Alexis's whereabouts were unknown. When he suddenly showed up in St. Petersburg in December, he installed his latest mistress, a coarse Finnish peasant named Afrosina, in his house. He ignored Charlotte, who suffered in silence. Her wing of the house was neglected to the point where rain began to come in through the roof. Ironically, considering his treatment of Alexis's mother, Peter angrily upbraided his son for neglecting his wife.

In October 1715, Charlotte gave birth to a son, who was named Peter. The difficult birth weakened the already depressed Charlotte, and she became ill. She refused treatment and died gratefully nine days later. The unhappy occasion was overshadowed by the birth of the czar's son, also named Peter. The royal birth was celebrated for a week in St. Petersburg. Alexis eagerly joined the festivities, and after the week was up he continued his dissolute ways and showed no interest in behaving like a future czar of Russia.

A few months later, Peter delivered "A Declaration to My Son," in which he told Alexis that if he did not change his ways, "I will deprive you of the succession, as one may cut off a useless member. Do not fancy that . . . I only write this to terrify you. I will certainly put it in execution if it please God; for whereas I do not spare my own life for my country and the welfare of my people, why should I spare you who do not render yourself worthy of either? I would rather choose to transmit them to a worthy stranger than to my own unworthy son." To his father's distress, Alexis immediately replied that he would gladly give up the succession if he could live out his life with Afrosina on a country estate. In January 1716, the czar sent a second ultimatum to his son: "Change your conduct and either strive to render yourself worthy of the succession or turn monk." Peter gave Alexis six months to come to a decision; in the meantime, the czar made another trip to western Europe.

Peter had several reasons for traveling. The recurring fevers and seizures that had plagued him for years seemed to be increasing in intensity and duration as he got older. He had neither slowed his frantic pace nor curbed his prodigious drinking, and he was advised by his worried doctors to go to Hanover to take the mineral-water cure. While in Germany, Peter also wanted to meet with his allies, Frederick William of Prussia, Frederick IV of Denmark, and George I, the elector of Hanover, to discuss possible ways of ending the war with Sweden.

Peter was worried about Charles, who had returned to Sweden and was now rattling his sword again, determined to regain his lost lands. With Charles back in command, Peter knew that the Swedes might once again become a formidable enemy. However, in 1715, Sweden's longtime ally, Louis XIV of France, died, and after many years of warfare, the French, it seemed, now sought peace. Part of the reason lay perhaps in the new king's inexperience and vulnerability: Louis XV was only

Catherine gave birth to a son, Peter, in 1715. After the czar denounced Alexis in 1718, young Peter became the heir to the throne, but he died in May 1719. The czar did not produce another heir.

Peter was delighted to meet the seven-year-old king of France, Louis XV, in the spring of 1717. The gigantic Russian playfully swept the little king up into the air — to the dismay of the French court.

seven years old. Peter made plans to visit France after Germany, and he looked forward to the trip, for France was the only major country he had missed during the Great Embassy.

The czar and several of his diplomatic entourage left Russia in January 1716. The Russians spent most of that year in Germany and Holland, discussing the Swedish problem with their allies. In early January 1717, Peter, laid up at The Hague with a high fever, received word that Catherine had borne another son, Paul. Just days later, the czar heard the sorrowful news that the infant Paul had died. More bad news quickly followed: Alexis's response to Peter's second ultimatum had been to flee Russia. He quickly disappeared, and all kinds of stories were being circulated.

Peter was incensed and embarrassed, but he managed to hold his temper. He ordered his envoys to conduct a quiet search for Alexis, and in May 1717 he left Holland for France. Despite his anxiety and the humiliation he felt at the thought that the French might know about Alexis, Peter was excited about seeing Paris. The day after Peter's arrival, the regent, the duc d'Orléans, paid him an official visit, and the two men talked for a few hours. Peter chafed to get out in the streets, but he uncharacteristically waited, according to French protocol, for the visit from the young king before he ventured out. Two days later, Louis XV arrived at Peter's suite. To the astonishment — and alarm — of the French, the czar swept the little boy into the air and kissed him several times. The young king kept his composure, however, and charmed his giant visitor with a short speech of welcome. After the French got over the initial shock of seeing their king held high in the air in the massive hands of the Russian monarch, they realized that Peter was, in fact, being most gracious and affectionate to the diminutive Louis.

The French court diarist, Louis de Rouvroy, duc de Saint-Simon, recorded his impressions of Peter, and his description provides an excellent picture of the czar at age 45. "One could not fail to perceive the air of greatness that was natural to him," Saint-Simon wrote. "In character, he was an extraordinary combination: He assumed majesty at its most regal, most proud, most unbending; yet, once his supremacy had been granted, his demeanor was infinitely gracious and full of discriminating courtesy. . . . He had a friendly approach which one associated with freedom, but he was not exempt from a strong imprint of his country's past. Thus his manners were abrupt, even violent, his wishes unpredictable, brooking no delay and no opposition."

In June, Peter left his ministers in France and returned to Amsterdam, where he took up the problem of Alexis. His son, it seemed, was hiding out with Afrosina in Naples, under the protection (ironically) of Charlotte's brother, Holy Roman Emperor Charles VI. The czar dispatched his shrewdest dip-

> *I do not think myself fit for government. . . . Therefore I do not aspire after you . . . to the succession of the Russian crown.*
>
> —CZAREVITCH ALEXIS
> to Peter the Great

Peter Tolstoy, the czar's most unscrupulous diplomat, was dispatched to Naples in June 1717 to bring back Alexis, who had been granted sanctuary from his father by Holy Roman Emperor Charles VI.

lomat, Peter Tolstoy, to Vienna. It did not take the Russian long to pressure the emperor into admitting that Alexis was in his empire. Tolstoy made his way to Naples, where he met with the errant czarevitch and delivered a letter from the czar. "If you are afraid of me," the czar had written, "I assure you and I promise to God and His judgment that I will not punish you. If you submit to my will by obeying me and if you return, I will love you better than ever."

Tolstoy held his tongue while Alexis mulled over the letter for two days. When the czarevitch declared that he still feared for his safety if he returned, Tolstoy belabored the young man mercilessly, telling him, among other things, that Peter would declare war on Austria if he did not return to Russia. Tolstoy also told the czarevitch that the emperor had withdrawn his support and that Peter himself was on his way to fetch him. This last bit of news nearly caused Alexis to faint. Finally, a thoroughly frightened and emotionally bruised Alexis agreed to return to Russia, but only if he was given a pardon and allowed to marry Afrosina and live with her on a country estate. Tolstoy relayed these demands to Peter, who acquiesced but stated that the marriage had to take place in Russia. Alexis was brought back to Russia. Afrosina, who was pregnant, returned later. There was no country estate waiting for them.

On February 3, 1718, in the Great Audience Hall of the Kremlin, an official assembly listened to the czar formally denounce and disinherit Alexis, who had submitted a written confession of his flight. The czar's two-year-old son, Peter, was proclaimed heir to the throne. The czar, convinced that a conspiracy existed and that Alexis was at the center of it, reneged on his promises and informed his son that only by naming all those who had assisted him in his flight would he receive a pardon. The desperate Alexis began naming names, and Peter ordered the arrest of anyone who had been even remotely friendly toward his son.

Peter had Alexis's mother brought from the Suzdal convent for questioning, and he arrested some of the nuns for sympathizing with her. When he discovered that Eudoxia had not exactly been living the life of a nun — she had taken her guard as a lover — the czar subjected the unfortunate man to torture to see if he harbored any traitorous ideas. He was among those who were publicly executed. Alexis's uncle, his servants, and his confessor were beheaded. Others, including the nuns, were whipped or knouted. But it was Afrosina — the woman Alexis loved so much and was prepared to give up so much for—who sealed his fate.

Afraid for her own life, Afrosina revealed all the venom Alexis had ever spewed out against his father. He had greeted happily the news that some soldiers had mutinied; he had not grieved over the illnesses of the czarevitch Peter. More damning were the political comments Alexis had made, usually when he was drunk: After the czar's death, Alexis would abandon St. Petersburg, proclaim Moscow the capital again, and return the clergy to its proper status. One remark in particular cut Peter to the quick: Alexis would dismantle the navy. Although these may have been only the idle and boastful remarks of a drunken and petulant man-child, Peter's fear that all his work might be undone by Alexis if

One of Alexis's tutors is arrested by the czar's secret police. Anyone suspected of aiding Alexis in his flight from Russia was apprehended and tortured.

Peter interrogates Alexis following his son's attempt to escape from Russia. Alexis was convicted of treason and imprisoned. Alexis died in prison — he was probably executed — on June 26, 1718.

he succeeded to the throne convinced the czar that Alexis was as much a threat as the streltsy had been. Peter ordered his son to stand trial for treason.

At a June 14 hearing, Peter presented the charges against Alexis. Alexis, bewildered by the faithless Afrosina and broken by torture, admitted his guilt. Peter instructed the judges to treat the czarevitch as any other man accused of treason. Accordingly, the court sentenced him to death for treason against czar and country. The sentence went to the czar for approval or commutation. Before Peter could give a decision, on the night of June 26, Alexis died in prison. The official report stated that after begging his father's forgiveness, the czarevitch had died in a fit of apoplexy, unable to bear the burden of his sins. But it is more likely that Peter had his son

executed in prison, in order to keep the brutal and ruthless deed away from the public eye.

The following day, Peter ordered the annual Poltava celebration held as usual. Even though Alexis had died a convicted traitor, Peter ordered that his son's body, now resting in a coffin draped in black velvet, lie in state in the Church of the Holy Trinity in St. Petersburg. On June 30, the czar and his ministers — who were forbidden to wear black mourning clothes — attended the small funeral. Then, carrying lighted candles, they followed the coffin to the Peter and Paul Cathedral, where Alexis was interred, next to the neglected Charlotte, in the new royal vault. There were reports that at the service for his dead son, Peter wept bitterly. Afrosina was pardoned.

8

Emperor of All the Russias

In May 1719, less than a year after the death of Alexis, the czar's little son, Peter, passed away. By now, Catherine and Peter had buried six children. The unhappy couple would see two more sons into the grave. They sought comfort in one another and tried to believe it was God's will that their children were taken. Still, after Alexis, the czar had pinned his hopes for the future on young Peter, and he took his son's death particularly hard; he could not help but feel that he was being punished for his treatment of Alexis. Not even Catherine could console the distraught Peter, who locked himself in his room and raged and wept for days. The entire senate gathered outside Peter's chamber door to talk him into coming out, for the country's sake. The members of the senate knew the impact of such an appeal, for service to his country was still the czar's driving force, and his country needed him now. His ministers were engaged in negotiations with Sweden to terminate their seemingly endless war, and Peter's formidable presence was essential if the Russians were to deal with Charles from a position of strength.

You have seen me punish the crimes of a son who was ungrateful, hypocritical, and malicious beyond all imagination. . . . By so doing I hope to have ensured the endurance of my great work, which is to make the Russian nation forever powerful and formidable.

—PETER THE GREAT
to his boyars, on
Alexis's trial

In 1721, Peter, 50 years old and in ill health, signed the Treaty of Nystad, thus ending the Great Northern War. The cessation of hostilities with Sweden allowed the czar to spend his final years concentrating on domestic reforms in Russia.

Although he was willing to give up some of the land won from Sweden, Peter was adamant about keeping the provinces that surrounded St. Petersburg. King Charles was equally determined to regain all the territory he had lost, and, moreover, he wanted Russia to pay an indemnity for starting the conflict. The negotiations dragged on interminably, and Peter had begun to despair of ever breaking the stalemate when he heard a startling report — King Charles of Sweden was dead.

Fittingly, the warrior-king of Sweden had died a soldier's death. While standing atop an earthen parapet during a siege of a castle in Norway, bold Charles had been shot through the head and died instantly. Peter realized that it was a fortuitous event for Russia; the Swedes did not have any leader comparable to Charles, and they were in no position now to challenge Peter. Yet the czar, who had always admired the king as a brilliant commander and a formidable foe, felt a sadness at the loss, as at the passing of an old friend, and he ordered his court into a week's mourning.

There was yet another obstacle to ending the war. King George I of England, who feared that the decline of Swedish power in the Baltic would lead to Russian control there, tried to intimidate Peter by sending a large fleet into the area. Exasperated, Peter ordered a naval campaign against Sweden. For five weeks, Russian ships harassed the eastern coast of Sweden, burning villages to the ground and deftly sailing away before the Swedish army could arrive. The swift Russian galleys easily outran the heavier, more cumbersome British warships, sometimes luring them into unfamiliar waters where the British would run aground. By the summer of 1720, King George had had enough, and he began to withdraw his fleet. In June 1721, after the Russians launched a third devastating campaign — by this time, Peter's ships had ravaged more than 400 miles of Swedish coastlands—the Swedes relented.

The Treaty of Nystad was signed on September 10, 1721. Peter was granted most of the land he wanted: Livonia, Ingria, Estonia, and most of Karelia. He returned much of the captured Finnish

This monarch [Peter] has brought our country to a level with others. He taught us to recognize that we are a people. Everything that we look upon in Russia has its origin in him, and everything which is done in the future will be derived from this source.

—IVAN NEPLUYEV
naval officer
and ambassador
to Constantinople

territory to Sweden, and prisoners on both sides were released. The end of the 21-year Great Northern War was joyously celebrated in Russia. In the streets of St. Petersburg, wine and beer were freely distributed while Peter announced the treaty from a platform. Toasting the Russian nation, Peter raised a colossal goblet to the thundering of cannon from the Peter and Paul Fortress. In October, the senate asked Peter to accept the title "Peter the Great, father of the country, emperor of all the Russias."

The czar, sword in hand, argues with Jacob Dolgoruky. The Russian senate lived in fear of Peter and would make no decision without his approval; Dolgoruky was one of the few men who were not frightened by Peter's rages.

Merchants and consumers gather at an outdoor market in Russia. Following the example of countries in Western Europe, Peter created conditions under which free enterprise flourished.

The dream Peter had nurtured ever since the days when he and his boyhood friends played at war in Preobrazhenskoe had become reality: Russia was now a major power on land and at sea, a nation to be respected — and feared. But Peter's vision of a new Russia had always included social, political, and economic vistas as well, vistas that were as yet unreached. So it was that during the final years of his life, Peter devoted most of his time and energy to reforming the government, economy, and social condition of his country.

The Russian senate, which Peter had created in 1711, was not functioning as the czar had planned. The indecisive senators wasted time arguing among

themselves and would not formulate decrees until told to by the czar. Peter found the body too slow, the senators too unwilling to make decisions. When the senate functioned at all, it was because of Jacob Dolgoruky, who even at 73 was a commanding figure, one of the few ministers who stood up to the czar. To give some direction to the senate, Peter appointed a procurator general, Pavel Yaguzhinsky, the son of a Lithuanian church organist. His job was to manage the senate, introduce legislation, see it through discussion, and send it before Peter for approval. He was also instructed to keep order among the senators and prevent arguments from getting overheated.

Peter had determined that a separate executive body was needed; he had observed the efficiency of the system of ministries in such countries as Prussia and Sweden. He therefore established nine new colleges: War, Admiralty, Foreign Affairs, Justice, Financial Control, Revenue Collection, Expenditure, Commerce, and Mining and Manufacturing. Most of the colleges had a Russian president and a foreign vice-president (to teach the Russians about administration). The colleges made a slow start. This type of government was not in the Russian tradition, and many new concepts of law and procedure had to be learned. Peter himself was a large part of the problem because he commanded officials to make decisions but punished them if they made the wrong ones. The new bodies did not know how to work independently of the czar, and most men did not want the responsibility of making a decision the czar would disapprove of. In his later years, when Peter realized this, he tried to give freer rein to the colleges to enable his officials to work on their own. Though the colleges eventually would be renamed ministries and the senate would become the Council of Empire, Peter's administrative structure

In his final years, the czar initiated a project to build a series of canals that would connect St. Petersburg to the Russian interior. Peter died before the construction could be completed.

would remain the basis of the Russian imperial government until its downfall in the Bolshevik Revolution of 1917.

The czar wanted to instill the idea that everyone, regardless of birth, could rise in the service of the state. In 1722 he created the Table of Ranks of the Russian Empire, which detailed three parallel systems of state service — civil, judicial, and military. Each system had 14 ranks, and every man entered service at the bottom. Good performance and length of service drew him up through the ranks, and middle- and even lower-class men could now rise to the status of "hereditary nobleman." The titles of the old aristocracy were not abolished, but they no longer represented the sole means to wealth and social status. For those men tenacious enough and talented enough, low birth was no longer an insurmountable barrier to the good life.

Determined to effect changes that would encourage trade and industry in Russia, Peter instituted economic reforms. His travels in western Europe had taught him that private enterprise was crucial to maintaining and stimulating a healthy economy. The czar decided to create a merchant class and an

atmosphere that was conducive to commercial enterprise by giving loans, tax breaks, and subsidies to nobles who started businesses. Because of the long war, heavy industry developed first and fastest. Under the guidance of the College of Mining and Manufacturing, a huge complex of iron and copper foundries was built in the Ural Mountains. Centered around the town of Ekaterinburg (named after Catherine), the factories were both state and privately owned, and they expanded rapidly. By the end of the century, Russia would become the largest iron producer in Europe.

To encourage commerce, Peter developed a fourfold plan: to make St. Petersburg a thriving trade port; to establish a system of canals connecting Russia's vast network of inland waterways with the Baltic Sea; to expand trade routes to the East; and to explore the huge interior, beyond the Urals, for exploitable natural resources. Peter gradually diverted trade from Arkhangel'sk to St. Petersburg, and as the European ships that had previously called at Arkhangel'sk went to St. Petersburg, Peter's pride and joy began to hum with the noise and flurry of a busy seaport. The czar's canal scheme was not fully realized, but a four-year effort resulted in a canal that linked the Volga and Neva rivers, thereby allowing goods to travel to and from the interior and the Baltic. Peter attempted to increase trade with China — Eastern goods, including silk and tea, were in great demand in Europe — but the Manchu rulers of China were suspicious of foreign involvement in their country and rebuffed Peter's overtures. In his attempt to redirect a trade route to India, Peter tried to establish control of the eastern shores of the Caspian Sea, but the Turks, who dominated the other side of the sea, remained hostile to any Russian presence there, and Peter was forced to abandon the idea.

Russian efforts in Siberia and along the Pacific coast were more successful. In 1710, Peter had made Siberia one of his first administrative provinces, and he promoted the timber and mining industries that made use of the region's vast natural

> *The establishment of the [Russian] empire is perhaps Europe's greatest event after the discovery of the New World.*
>
> —VOLTAIRE
> 17th-century
> French philosopher

resources. The czar also claimed the Kamchatka Peninsula and the Kuril Islands, north of Japan. In 1724, Peter hired Danish-born Vitus Bering to explore the lands beyond Kamchatka. Although Peter died before learning the results of this venture, Bering would discover the narrow strait separating Russia from North America that would allow for Russian exploration and, eventually, settlement of lands stretching from Alaska to as far south as San Francisco.

Despite Peter's encouragement of industry and commerce, Russia remained a predominantly rural, agricultural country — in 1700 fewer than five percent of the population lived in towns and cities. Many of Peter's reforms had little impact on the Russian peasants; others, such as compulsory military service, were widely felt and widely hated. Perhaps the greatest change in the life of the people came with his tax reforms. Until a wider economic base could be built in Russia, the only way to increase state revenue was to increase taxes, and the Russian people were taxed almost beyond endurance. Taxes were collected on households, and in rural Russia, when the tax collector came around, entire families

The squalid and overcrowded interior of a Russian peasants' dwelling. Peter's many economic reforms improved the quality of life for everyone in Russia except the peasantry.

would vanish from their houses. Sometimes even the houses, flimsy, one-room shacks, easily assembled and taken apart, would vanish also, and the tax collector would return empty-handed.

During his visit to France, Peter had seen the value of a head tax, which counted individuals, not households. In 1722 he ordered a census taken, and then he instituted the "soul tax." Every Russian adult male was now responsible for paying taxes. Noblemen, merchants, and the clergy were not included in the soul census because they were taxed separately. From Peter's viewpoint, the soul tax was a huge success: It produced half the state revenue for 1724. However, it contributed to the growing enslavement of the masses. Serfs and free peasants made up 95 percent of the population. Up until now, the Russian serf had been bound to the land he worked; he was not an individual piece of property to be bought or sold separately from the land. Under Peter's soul tax, however, the landlords became responsible for paying taxes based on the census count. The new system thus gave landlords more control over the lives of their peasants. Instead of being tied to the land, the serfs and peasants were now bound to the person of the landlord. In 1722, Peter decreed that serfs could not leave their estates without written permission from their landlords. The oppression of the Russian peasant thus certified by Peter was to eventually play a major part in the bloody downfall of the czarist system in Russia.

Peter also reformed the religious establishment in Russia. The czar was not interested in changing matters of faith. What he did want was to control the church administration — to make it, in essence, a compliant branch of the state — and to rid the church of its putrid baggage of idle, corrupt, and ignorant priests. There were over 500 monasteries and convents in Russia; many of them enjoyed extraordinary wealth, and the czar felt that too many monks lived in unseemly luxury. Peter had initiated his church reforms in 1700, when Patriarch Adrian, the head of the Orthodox church, died suddenly. Peter seized the opportunity to create the Monastery Office, which would regulate the number of monks and control the finances of the monasteries.

> *One might go on forever describing this truly great man with his remarkable character and rare variety of extraordinary talents. They will make him a monarch worthy of profound admiration for countless years.*
>
> —SAINT-SIMON
> French court
> diarist, on Peter

In 1721, Peter announced the Ecclesiastical Regulation, which replaced the patriarchate with the Holy Governing Synod. The synod acted much as Peter's colleges of administration, with a lay officer appointed to ensure that it ran smoothly. Members of the clergy were required to take an oath of loyalty to the czar. To rid the priesthood of its rampant ignorance and superstition, Peter ordered the clergy's education to encompass such subjects as history, politics, and science. Peter's church reform thoroughly subordinated the Russian Orthodox church to the state. The church, which had enjoyed an independent authority equal to that of the czars', evolved into an agency of support for the czar, and it became so closely identified with the imperial government that it came crashing down with it in 1917.

Peter succeeded in subjugating the once-powerful Russian Orthodox church during his reign. By the time of his death in 1725, the church had become another arm of the state apparatus.

During the last few years of his life, Peter was increasingly ill. With no heir, the question of succession weighed heavily on him. Shortly before he died, realizing that he would not produce a male heir, Peter abolished the old father-to-son succession law and declared that every czar would henceforward choose his own successor. In May 1724, dressed in a light blue tunic with red silk stockings, Peter accompanied Catherine, who wore a purple gown trimmed in gold, to the Cathedral of the Assumption in Moscow. Placing upon Catherine's head a new crown of 2,500 diamonds, pearls, and other precious gems, topped by an enormous ruby on a diamond cross, Peter officially proclaimed his wife empress of Russia.

That summer, Peter's illness surfaced in a particularly severe form, and the czar suffered agonizing waves of pain. In November, after jumping into the icy Neva to help rescue the passengers of a capsized boat, Peter took to his bed with a fever. The czar never fully recovered, and by mid-January the illness was so advanced that his doctors feared internal gangrene had set in. A distraught Catherine sat by her husband's bedside, imploring God to release him from his pain. Peter tried to give instructions before slipping into delirium, writing, "Give all

Wracked by fevers, Peter the Great died on February 8, 1725. Construction of a statue in his honor was begun more than 50 years later.

to. . .”; but the sentence remained unfinished. On the morning of February 8, 1725, Peter the Great, emperor of all the Russias, died. He was buried near Alexis in St. Petersburg — even in death the czar's unhappy son could not escape his father's long shadow. The grieving widow became Empress Catherine I.

Peter's fears that his reforms would not outlast him proved unfounded. Russia was now permanently oriented toward the West, and it continued to develop in the direction he had envisioned. Peter had dragged his country into the light of the modern world, and there it would remain, for better or for worse. By personal example — and through brute force — he had taught his subjects the concept of a Russian nation. Peter has been both venerated for his spectacular achievements and denounced for his brutality and oppression of the Russian people. It is true that Peter's accomplishments — the army and navy, St. Petersburg, the government, the economic growth — could not have been realized without the huge sacrifice of the Russian people. It is equally true that those achievements would not have come about without Peter's singular vision and the sheer force of his will.

Further Reading

Klyuchevsky, Vasili. *Peter the Great.* Translated by Liliana Archibald. Boston: Beacon Press, 1984.

Massie, Robert K. *Peter the Great: His Life and World.* New York: Knopf, 1981.

Milner-Gulland, Robin, and Nikolai Dejevsky. *Cultural Atlas of Russia.* New York: Facts on File, 1989.

Pipes, Richard. *Russia Under the Old Regime.* New York: Macmillan, 1974.

Putnam, Peter Brock. *Peter, the Revolutionary Tsar.* New York: Harper & Row, 1973.

Raef, Marc. *Peter the Great Changes Russia.* 2nd ed. Lexington, MA: Heath, 1972.

Riasanovsky, Nicholas V. *A History of Russia.* 4th ed. New York: Oxford University Press, 1984.

———. *The Image of Peter the Great in Russian History and Thought.* New York: Oxford University Press, 1985.

Sumner, Benedict H. *Peter the Great and the Emergence of Russia.* New York: Macmillan, 1962.

Troyat, Henri. *Peter the Great: A Biography.* Translated by Joan Pinkham. New York: Dutton, 1987.

Chronology

May 30, 1672	Born Peter Alekseyevich to Czar Alexis I and his second wife, Natalya Naryshkina
1682	Czar Fyodor dies; Peter and his half-brother Ivan become co-czars; first streltsy revolt; Sophia Miloslavskaya becomes regent
1688	Peter marries Eudoxia Lopukhina
1689	Wrests political control from Sophia and rules with Ivan
Feb. 1690	Czarevitch Alexis is born
June 1695	Peter's first attack on Turkish stronghold of Azov fails
1696	Czar Ivan dies; Peter conquers Azov; building of the Southern Fleet commences
1697–98	Great Embassy
1698–99	Second streltsy revolt; Peter crushes streltsy; initiates the westernization of Russia
1700	Great Northern War begins; Peter declares war on Sweden; Charles XII defeats Russians at Narva
1702	Russian conquest of Noteborg, Dorpat, and Narva
May 1702	Founding of St. Petersburg
1705–8	Peter crushes Cossack rebellions in southern Russia
1708	Charles XII invades Russia
June 28, 1709	Battle of Poltava
1711	Ottoman Empire declares war on Russia; Peter defeated at Prut River
Feb. 19, 1712	Peter marries Catherine in public ceremony
August 1714	Russian victory at Hangö
Jan. 7, 1717	Alexis flees Russia
May 1717	Peter visits Paris
June 1718	Trial and death of Czarevitch Alexis
1719	Charles XII killed
Sept. 1721	Treaty of Nystad ends Great Northern War
May 1724	Catherine is crowned empress
Feb. 8, 1725	Peter the Great dies

Index

Kathleen McDermott received her M.A. in Slavic languages from the University of California, Los Angeles. A former assistant editor for Chelsea House Publishers, she does free-lance writing and editing in New York City, is an avid student of Russian and East European history, and is currently associate editor for the History Book Club.

Arthur M. Schlesinger, jr., taught history at Harvard for many years and is currently Albert Schweitzer Professor of the Humanities at City University of New York. He is the author of numerous highly praised works in American history and has twice been awarded the Pulitzer Prize. He served in the White House as special assistant to Presidents Kennedy and Johnson.